THE FIRST-YEAR
Seminar

Designing, Implementing and Assessing Courses to Support Student Learning and Success

Instructor Training and Development
Volume Two

James E. Groccia
and Mary Stuart Hunter

NATIONAL RESOURCE CENTER
FIRST-YEAR EXPERIENCE® AND STUDENTS IN TRANSITION
UNIVERSITY OF SOUTH CAROLINA

Cite as:

Groccia, J. E., & Hunter, M. S. (2012). *The first-year seminar: Designing, implementing and assessing courses to support student learning and success: Vol. II. Instructor training and development.* Columbia, SC: University of South Carolina, National Resource Center for The First-Year Experience & Students in Transition.

Production Staff for the National Resource Center:

Series Editor	Tracy L. Skipper, Assistant Director for Publications
Project Editor	Dottie Weigel, Editor
Design and Production	Melody Taylor, Graphic Artist

Library of Congress Cataloging-in-Publication Data
Keup, Jennifer R.
  The first-year seminar : designing, implementing, and assessing courses to support student learning & success / Jennifer R. Keup and Joni Webb Petschauer.
     p. cm.
  Includes bibliographical references.
  ISBN 978-1-889271-76-7
  1. College freshmen--United States. 2. College student orientation--United States. 3. Interdisciplinary approach in education--United States. I. Petschauer, Joni Webb. II. Title.
  LB2343.32.K48 2011
  378.1'98--dc22
                    2011015354

Contents

List of Figures

Notes on the Series

As I introduce the second volume in this comprehensive series on designing, implementing, and assessing first-year seminars, I hope the readers will indulge me in a moment of personal reflection. I have been teaching at the college level for about 13 years now. Prior to going back to graduate school for a degree in English, I worked in student affairs. In this capacity, I *taught* students in a variety of situations—resident assistant training, roommate mediation sessions, disciplinary hearings, academic advising appointments, just to name a few. My training and professional experience in student affairs gave me a solid understanding of how college students learn and develop. I certainly was not a novice educator, but when I walked into that first composition class and took my place at the front of the classroom, I was keenly aware of my amateur status. To be sure, much of my discomfort was due to having to teach a subject that I myself was still trying to master. And despite the clear emphasis on collaborative learning and shared authority in the literature on composition pedagogy, I was still strongly influenced by the received notion that the instructor should be the master and commander of that classroom ship.

During my graduate studies, I also taught the first-year seminar at the University of South Carolina a couple of times. Here, I did not struggle with the content—my student affairs work had prepared me to address the more common topics in the seminar—but I did struggle with the emphasis on process. I was still very much a white-knuckle kind of instructor, holding on to the podium as if my life depended on it. I lacked the confidence in my own teaching—and perhaps in my students—to let them take the reins.

Back in the English classroom these days, I still experience moments of anxiety, driven by the notion that I need to be in charge. While I cannot claim that my classroom is completely learner-centered, I do try to give students more control of the learning experience. When I teach a course on critical reading and writing, I select the readings for the first month or so and then let the students pick what we read for the rest of the semester. In my course on teaching writing at the high school level, I share instructional responsibilities with the students, asking them to present mini writing lessons in which I participate as a student with the rest of the class and to guide our discussion of the readings. Early one semester, students raised concerns about the common practice of asking students to write proposals in advance of final projects. Since that was an assignment on my syllabus, I spent part of a class asking students to help me design an alternate assignment that better served their needs and learning styles while still achieving some of the basic goals for the course. In all of my courses, I ask students to give me some informal feedback about halfway through the class, and I make adjustments based on what they tell me.

That I struggled during my first few years of teaching is not a unique story. In fact, I suspect it is an all-too common story on our campuses. Just like our students, any time we step into a new role, we are likely to experience some minor bumps during the transition. My challenges in the classroom resulted from concerns both about content mastery and delivery of instruction. As Jim Groccia and Stuart Hunter suggest in this volume, these twin concerns provide the impetus for faculty development initiatives for first-year seminars. The content for first-year seminars frequently includes topics that influence student learning, development, and success, such as campus involvement, major and career selection, substance abuse, sexuality and sexual relationships, health and wellness, and so on. Faculty may feel ill-equipped to address these topics with college students, especially if there is not a natural connection to their discipline. Some first-year seminars focus on a disciplinary topic of the instructor's choosing. In those cases, faculty may feel less anxiety about the content; however, the student-centered, process-focused nature of the seminar may present challenges to their preferred instructional strategies.

The first-year seminar was explicitly designed to help students navigate the social and academic transitions to the college environment. But it is important to recognize that the first-year students may not be the only ones undergoing a transition here. If the course is to be successful, we must also support educators—faculty and administrators—in their transition to first-year seminar instruction. Obviously, the first step in that transition would be some type of in-depth training experience exploring the goals of the course, recommended content, the nature of students enrolled in the course, and strategies for instruction. Yet, as is the case with new students entering college, intensive, one-shot learning experiences are necessary but not sufficient to support long-term success. New instructors need ongoing opportunities to learn about the course, to discuss their challenges, and to receive feedback on their performance. Veteran instructors of the seminar need exposure to new content areas and pedagogies. As such, this volume offers advice for designing initial training opportunities for seminar instructors and implementing ongoing faculty development initiatives.

We hope this volume offers ample guidance in designing and redesigning faculty development initiatives in support of first-year seminars. We also hope that readers will find inspiration for more generalized faculty training programs. As the authors have drawn from the larger discussion of training and development, much of the advice here could encompass a campus-wide approach to training instructors that was inclusive of the first-year seminar. Such a comprehensive approach to faculty training and development would mean that my story would become much less common on American college campuses. And that would be a very good thing—for both students and those who teach them.

As always, we welcome your feedback on this volume and on the larger series of which it is a part.

Tracy L. Skipper
Series Editor
National Resource Center for The First-Year Experience & Students in Transition
University of South Carolina

Introduction

We have heard it said time and again, that first-year seminar programs are only as strong the instructors who teach in them and the instructor development initiatives that undergird them. Yet, 20.8% of respondents to the 2009 National Survey of First-Year Seminars reported that instructor training was not offered on their campuses (Padgett & Keup, 2011). Of those offering training, only half required it. Because the first-year seminar is a relatively new discipline in higher education, many, if not most, of the instructors teaching these courses today did not take the seminar during their own collegiate experience and therefore lack personal experience with the goals, methods, and management of such courses. For that reason among many others, preparing instructors for teaching first-year seminars can be a challenging but necessary undertaking.

This book is the second in a multi-volume series focusing on designing, implementing, and assessing first-year seminars. Each volume looks at a different aspect of seminar design or administration and offers suggestions for practice grounded in the literature on teaching and learning, research on first-year seminars, and campus-based examples. As an outgrowth of the University 101 course at the University of South Carolina, the National Resource Center for The First-Year Experience and Students in Transition is firmly grounded in faculty development initiatives, having sponsored workshops and published resources on the topic throughout its 30-year history. In fact, this is the third publication from the National Resource Center on instructor development for first-year seminar programs. The first publication was a short 18-page booklet, *Freshman Seminar Instructor Training: Guidelines for Design and Implementation* by John N. Gardner, published by the Center in 1992. The booklet, now out of print, was written in the form of questions and answers, addressing such basics as the rationale for instructor training; the scheduling and frequency of training events; identification and selection of facilitators; and organizational, conceptual, and content considerations. Then in 1999, Mary Stuart Hunter and Tracy L. Skipper edited *Solid Foundations: Building Success for First-Year Seminars Through Instructor Training and Development*. This monograph, also out of print, offered a research-based rationale for implementing an instructor training program and described potential content and organization of instructor training programs. Thus, this third publication on first-year seminar instructor development from the National Resource Center revisits the topics in the earlier publications, while also for the first time in book format, providing attention to evaluation as a critical element in instructor development. The theoretical foundations of faculty development and teaching and learning initiatives that inform first-year seminar instructor preparation and ongoing support are also central topics. The treatment of faculty development in this publication focuses on instruction in first-year seminars. As such, the reader will see many parallels between aspects of faculty development and the content and pedagogy of the first-year seminar.

The volume opens by making a case for an ongoing commitment to instructor development in chapter 1. We begin with a broad treatment of the current educational context and the critical student learning outcomes for the 21st century. Higher education, beginning with first-year courses, will play a central role in meeting this century's economic, political, and social realities for both students and the larger global society. Obviously, college teaching is a primary factor in achieving these goals, and this chapter makes the case for an ongoing commitment to faculty development programs. We also describe the connection between teaching, engagement, and student persistence and how faculty development initiatives can help campuses achieve institutional retention goals. After providing the history and context of faculty development as an important undertaking in the academy, we define it and offer a learning cycle as a model for planning and implementing initiatives.

Chapter 2 provides a basic overview of planning and organizing faculty development programs. It addresses a strategic approach to developing first-year seminar instructor training efforts and offers suggestions for continuous faculty development training and shorter term, even one-shot, programs. Elements of successful instructor training programs are offered and potential formats are described. The chapter concludes with an important discussion of evaluating training initiatives.

Designing successful training and development programs is dependent on many variables including institutional context and traditions, trainer expertise and experience, goals of the training program, level of teaching preparation and experience of the seminar instructors, and availability of resources. The fact that there is no single *right* way to design and deliver training for first-year seminar instructors is both challenging and freeing. Yet, understanding how people learn is a common and foundational aspect of designing and delivering quality instructor development initiatives. Chapter 3 addresses assumptions related to adult learning and delves into a summary of important findings that can help designers better understand the dynamics of learning. Thus, the process of learning is central to this chapter.

Chapter 4 opens with a framework for determining training content by considering learning outcomes, instructor variables, learner variables, learning processes, learning context, course content, and instructional processes. The chapter also addresses some specific topics important for instructor training related to the first-year seminar, including student development theory, learning goals for first-year students, institutional context, and content sequencing. In the first-year seminar, the learning process is frequently as, if not more, important as the content of the course. In this way, the *process* of teaching the seminar becomes important content for instructor development events. To this end, the chapter describes a variety of teaching strategies that can be used in professional development events to serve as models for the seminar classroom.

Chapter 5 addresses evaluation as a critical, yet often untapped resource, for instructor development. Encouraging reflection and providing feedback to individual instructors is a valuable way to enhance their teaching abilities. This chapter offers a detailed description for using instructor evaluation as a developmental tool to promote faculty growth.

The first five chapters offer guidance on designing instructor development initiatives, and in chapter 6, we move in a slightly different direction, exploring approaches for building and maintaining a dedicated instructional corps for the first-year seminar. The first part of the chapter focuses on recruiting new instructors to teach first-year seminars, outlining desired instructor characteristics and ideas for identifying pools of, and strategies for recruiting, potential instructors. Yet, first-year seminar directors also understand that successful recruitment is not sufficient to sustain a quality program. Faculty development does not end when the semester begins. As such, the chapter explores factors that motivate instructors to begin (and continue) teaching in the seminar and addresses strategies for cultivating ongoing relationships with seminar instructors through community building, communication, and involvement in program evaluation and improvement efforts.

The volume concludes in chapter 7 with a series of recommendations from the authors for those who embrace the potential of faculty development to create and sustain highly effective first-year seminar programs.

It is our hope that this volume will provide a rich resource for program leadership who desire to begin or enhance existing faculty development programs for first-year seminars. Perhaps with this resource, the numbers of institutions offering and requiring training for first-year seminar instructors will rise substantially before the next administration of the National Survey of First-Year Seminars.

A wide variety of potential uses for this volume exist. It can be used as a cookbook for first-year seminar program directors as they envision and plan faculty development activities. The various charts, models, and lists can be used to benchmark efforts on a particular campus. Other potential uses include a supplemental reading for graduate or continuing education courses on first-year experience topics. It can also be used for those interested in faculty development in general as an example of the application of such initiatives in a particular setting. Regardless of how the volume is used, the authors hope that exposure to new ideas will help readers gain valuable insights that can be applied in their campus-based programs or, perhaps, offer reinforcement and validation for current practices.

Chapter 1
The Need for Instructor Training and Development

In *High Noon: Twenty Global Issues, Twenty Years to Solve Them,* Rischard (2002) suggests that because the new world economy is highly knowledge-intensive, one must be good at constantly learning. If one stands still, in reality, one falls back. As the world shrinks and becomes "flatter" (Friedman, 2007, p. 289)—the result of economic interdependence, global competition, and expanding communication technology—higher education becomes more critical for citizens of all countries around the world. Similarly, higher education plays a central role in finding solutions to critical global issues facing future generations worldwide. Thus, the quality of higher education and the need to facilitate high-level learning has never been more important (Groccia, 2010).

Higher education's challenge both in terms of content and pedagogy is to become more relevant to current and future needs. According to *College Learning for the New Global Century: A Report From the National Leadership Council for Liberal Education & America's Promise* (AAC&U, 2007), colleges and universities stand at a crossroads where millions of learners are entering a higher education system that requires reassessment and refocusing of teaching methods and learning outcomes to face the demands of new global realities. To be maximally relevant to this new world, higher education must recognize and attain essential learning outcomes that integrate liberal education values, methods, and content across the entire spectrum of academic disciplines. As the world is reshaped by scientific and technological innovations, global interdependence, cross-cultural contacts, and changes in economic and political power balances, the goals of higher education must also change (AAC&U). In the face of these shifting future realities, instructors must be supported to initiate curricular changes that prepare all learners for new 21st century challenges, including

» Knowledge of human cultures and the physical and natural world through study in the sciences, mathematics, social sciences, humanities, histories, languages, and the arts;

» Intellectual and practical abilities, including inquiry and analysis, critical and creative thinking, written and oral communication, quantitative and information literacy, and teamwork and problem-solving skills, by engagement with big, timely, and enduring questions;

» Personal and social responsibility, including civic knowledge and engagement, intercultural knowledge and competence, ethical reasoning and action, and foundations and skills for lifelong learning that is practiced across the curriculum through challenging problems and projects;

» Integrative learning, including synthesis and advanced study across both general and specialized study demonstrated through the application of knowledge, skills, and responsibilities to new settings and complex problems (AAC&U, p. 3).

However, the majority of faculty members, including, in some cases, those who teach first-year seminars receive little or no training in effective college-level teaching prior to assuming their academic appointments. When asked what was lacking in their teaching preparation, faculty members identify interacting with students and assessing learning, among the most glaring omissions (Sagendorf, 2007). These are essential elements of successful instruction, especially in the first year of college. Collaborative and cross-disciplinary teaching skills are often central elements of first-year courses and seminars. Yet, new faculty members have limited, if any, experience in these areas (Nyquist & Woodford, 2000). Additionally, many first-year seminars are taught by other campus employees not academically prepared for college-level teaching (e.g., academic advisors, librarians, student affairs administrators). Thus, the need to train a range of educators to teach the first-year seminar is critically important.

For new and early career instructors, teaching and course design usually come at the expense of time that can be devoted to research. When this happens, many instructors revert to using what they know and have successfully experienced as learners—the lecture—as the primary, perhaps only, teaching method. This means that often introductory and lower-level courses, those most frequently taken by first-year students, often do not incorporate engaged learning strategies (National Research Council, 2003), and novice instructors, at least initially, are likely to continue to lecture. Some change does appear to be taking place in terms of increasing use of nonlecture teaching techniques (see DeAngelo et al., 2009). For new instructors with little prior experience and knowledge about teaching and learning, students become subjects in a teaching experiment where learning outcomes are subject to the trials and errors of on the job training—a potentially unethical but not uncommon situation (Sagendorf, 2007).

While no data are available on the percentage of instructors who have had formal training, the authors' experiences in providing teaching consultations and workshops suggest that number is no more than half. Compounding the problem of inadequate teaching preparation is the fact that most instructors do little to improve their teaching skills once employed in collegiate settings. The authors' best estimate from the review of annual reports of teaching and learning centers posted on center websites or obtained from center directors as well as personal conversations, indicates that only 20-40% of instructional staff (including graduate teaching assistants) use campus faculty development services. Based on attendance figures at teaching workshops where the authors have worked, it is estimated that even fewer nontraditional instructors, such as those who come from administrative and student affairs positions and teach first-year seminars, participate in optional or elective teaching enhancement activities.

This chapter offers a rationale for institutionalizing instructor training and development for the first-year seminar in particular but also for the college as a whole. These concepts are based on the student engagement and retention literature demonstrating the importance of excellence in teaching to student learning, persistence, and success. The authors also explore the history and context of faculty development in American colleges and universities and offer a series of definitions guiding work in this area today. The chapter concludes with a model of a faculty development learning cycle, which sets the stage for the rest of the volume.

The Need to Engage Learners

Each of the essential learning outcomes identified by AAC&U (2007) in *College Learning for the New Global Century* requires instructional staff to develop effective educational practices that engage students across disciplinary boundaries in learning experiences that tackle real problems, allow for the application of course content to those problems, and lead to sustained intellectual growth and a heightened sense of personal responsibility. The report calls on educational leaders to "expand substantially investments in active, hands-on, collaborative, and inquiry-based forms of teaching and learning—making full use of new educational technologies—to ensure that all learners have rich opportunities" to achieve 21st century learning goals (p. 11).

The need to create engaged learning environments and opportunities has also been highlighted by the National Survey of Student Engagement:

> What students *do* during college counts more in terms of desired outcomes than who they are or even where they go to college. That is, the voluminous research on college student development shows that the time and energy students devote to educationally purposeful activities is the single best predictor of their learning and personal development (Astin, 1993; Pace, 1980; Pascarella & Terenzini, 1991). (Kuh, 2003, p. 1, original emphasis)

Whether the learner is a first-year student of any age, a student at any other point in their formal education experience, or a first-year seminar instructor in a training experience, engagement has three levels: the behavioral, affective, and cognitive. The behavioral level represents what learners do—the degree of participation, effort, and persistence that they demonstrate in an activity. Levels of interest, motivation, and enjoyment signify the affective component of engagement (i.e., how learners feel and the level of attachment and commitment they express in the activity). The cognitive level of engagement represents the degree of mental activity and processing or elaboration that is stimulated by an activity. The ability of individual instructors and the institution as a whole to engage learners on these three levels (i.e., doing, feeling, and thinking) will contribute to educational experiences that lead to higher level learning, retention, and satisfaction.

Figure 1.1, a modification of Groccia's (2004) model illustrates the many ways that student learners can be engaged on each of these three levels during their academic experience. For example, engagement with faculty and staff suggests that opportunities be supported for learners to participate with instructors in such things as undergraduate research experiences, curricular development activities, tutorials, professional activities (e.g., attending professional conferences and meetings), as well as having contact with instructors who serve as advisors to honor societies and academic and social clubs. Instructor participation in cocurricular activities and learning communities are other ways to foster engagement.

Figure 1.1. A model of learner engagement. Adapted from *Creating Engaged Learning Environments for Today's Students*, by J. Burns, J. Groccia, S. Hamid, and C. Staley, 2004, Teleconference produced by the National Resource Center for The First-Year Experience and Students in Transition. Copyright 2004 by James E. Groccia.

Engagement with other learners suggests that students be encouraged to create community with others in residence halls as well as seminar contexts through the use of learning teams and learning communities, study groups, peer tutors, intramural sports, or academic clubs and societies. There is ample evidence (Debard & Sacks, 2010) that social fraternities and sororities encourage engagement and contribute to satisfaction and retention.

Students can be integrated into teaching activities functioning as peer teaching assistants, peer mentors, peer tutors, or undergraduate grading assistants. According to McKeachie and Svinicki (2006), "the best answer to the question 'What is the most effective method of teaching?' is that it depends on the goal, the student, the content, and the teaching. The next best answer may be 'students teaching other students'" (p. 214). First-year seminars, which often facilitate greater learner engagement by using discussions and group projects as opposed to traditional lecture, engage students in teaching one another in both formal and informal ways. Miller, Groccia, and Miller (2001) present more than 30 examples of ways that faculty in different disciplines from universities around the world have integrated undergraduate learners as instructional assistants.

Activities that move learners from passive recipients of knowledge to active participants in elaborating, discussing, sharing, questioning, and problem solving increases motivation and learning (Bonwell & Eison, 1991; Hake, 1998). Cooperative/collaborative group learning, problem-based learning, jigsaw learning activities, learning cells, individual and group projects, critical thinking activities, case studies, think-pair-share (for descriptions of these and other active learning techniques see Nilson, 2010; Silberman, 1996; Svinicki & McKeachie , 2010) and the use of remote response systems (i.e., clickers) are teaching techniques that more fully engage learners in their own and their peer's learning.

Developing teaching techniques that engage students with organizations and individuals in the community beyond the institution can enhance learning. First-year seminars offer a prime setting to introduce the concepts of campus engagement and integrated learning to new students. Using service activities to support in-class learning is effective and often supports the development of a sense of civic responsibility that encourages a life-long habit of service among participants.

Students can be encouraged to engage in undergraduate research and inquiry activities. Lopatto (2004) cites a number of studies that highlight the following positive impacts of engagement in undergraduate research: (a) increased interest in careers in the science, technology, engineering, and mathematics; (b) increased persistence in the pursuit of an undergraduate degree; (c) increased levels of pursuit of graduate education; (d) alumni retrospective reports of higher gains than comparison groups in skills such as carrying out research, acquiring information, and speaking effectively; (e) increased retention rate of minority undergraduates; and (f) increased rate of graduate education for minority students.

Connections Between Good Teaching and Student Success and Persistence

Good teaching matters for first-year student persistence, and participation in quality faculty development experiences can assist instructors in honing their skills. Active, engaged teaching practices, in addition to increasing learning, directly and indirectly affect college attrition (Braxton, Jones, Hirschy, & Hartley, 2008; Braxton, Milem, & Sullivan 2000). Social integration fostered by discussion and other active-learning techniques is positively associated with retention for first-year students: the more instructors use active-learning practices, the more learners feel that the institution is committed to their welfare. This perceived commitment is connected to future persistence (Braxton et al., 2008). Braxton et al. (2008) suggest that institutions encourage instructional improvement activities focusing on helping instructors expand skill in active-learning methods.

Pascarella, Seifert, and Whitt (2008) highlight the role of effective classroom instruction on learner persistence, especially from the first to second year. The results of a longitudinal study of first-year learners conducted by these authors suggest that overall exposure to organized and clear instruction seems to have positive net effects on the probability of returning for the second year of study. In addition, they report that learners exposed to instructors who teach in clear and organized ways are likely to be more confident and relaxed about their academic achievement. As such, the results of this study support the need for continued faculty and instructor development. Moreover, instructors can learn effective instructional behaviors by engaging in activities to improve their teaching. Yet, instructors need help moving beyond the lecture, the instructional method used by the majority of college teachers (Finkelstein, Seal, & Schuster, 1998). For some, this will be a foreign concept, as their own experience as learners was purely as recipients of lecture methods of instruction.

History and Context of Faculty Development

Faculty and instructor development has long been part of higher education, but such efforts were limited in scope until the 1960s (Gillespie, Hilson, & Wadsworth, 2002). Traditional interpretations of the term *faculty development* up until the 1970s meant sabbaticals, research grants, or funding to attend professional meetings. More recently, faculty development has been defined as an "institutional process which seeks to modify the attitudes, skills, and behavior of faculty members toward greater competence and effectiveness in meeting learner needs, their own needs, and the needs of the institution" (Francis, 1975, p. 720). In the United States, faculty development is widely used as an umbrella term that includes systematic efforts to increase the effectiveness of faculty members in the performance of all of their professional roles (Lewis, 1996) and that covers a wide range of activities (POD Network, 2011a).

In the United States, the forces that stimulated the rise of faculty and instructor development programs in the 1960s and 1970s were similar to those that fostered the creation of first-year experience programs; namely, student protests against poor, uninspired teaching, academic disengagement, and dissatisfaction with irrelevant courses (Gaff & Simpson, 1994). At the same time, expanded educational access increased the diversity of U.S. campuses with older, part-time, and culturally and racially heterogeneous populations replacing the ethnic, gender, and age homogeneity of past generations. This demographic shift challenged faculty and institutions to be innovative in ways that kept learners engaged and interested (Gaff & Simpson). The University 101 course at the University of South Carolina was introduced in 1972 as an educational experiment in response to 1970 student riots against the Vietnam War, other perceived social injustices, and local campus issues. The primary goal of the course was to build trust; understanding; and open lines of communication among students, faculty, staff, and administrators. Central to these early efforts was the creation of a major faculty development initiative to improve teaching in all undergraduate courses, not just the first-year seminar (University 101, n.d.).

Financial pressures exerted by the economic recession of the 1970s also challenged institutions to focus on maximizing the skills of current instructors rather than pursuing the past practices of *buying* almost unlimited numbers of faculty from other institutions (Lewis, 1996). Another outcome of the economic downturn of the mid-1970s was a reduction in instructor mobility from one institution to another, highlighting the need for colleges and universities to create programs to enhance the instructional knowledge and skills of their faculty.

Since the 1980s faculty and instructor development has emerged as a major conceptual force in higher education (Mathis, 1981). Figure 1.2 describes a model of academic work that extends the commonly accepted tripartite model (i.e., three-legged stool) of teaching, research, and service to include outreach and continuous professional development and improvement. Outreach differs from service in that it requires the application of one's disciplinary knowledge and expertise to problems and situations outside an instructor's normal institutional context. Service, on the other hand, can best be described as activities one performs to be a good academic citizen, such as sitting on the departmental admission committee or campus governing committees. More important for the current discussion, is that these authors believe that every instructor should be required, recognized, and rewarded for involving themselves in each of the five functions—teaching, research, outreach, service, and faculty development. Time and resources should be provided to enable instructors to refine their skills in each area.

Primary Dimensions of Faculty Work

1. Teaching _____
2. Research _____
3. Service _____
4. Outreach _____
5. Faculty Development _____

TOTAL: 100%

Figure 1.2. Primary dimensions of academic work.

Figure 1.2 can be helpful to faculty and those teaching first-year seminars as a planning and time management document. At the beginning of each academic year or instructional cycle, instructors could meet with their supervisors to develop their individual work plan allocating time in each of these five dimensions. Then, at the end of this period, actual effort and time spent in each category can be assessed and used as part of the evaluation process.

Faculty Development Definitions

Faculty and instructor development actually consists of three major areas: (a) *individual development,* (b) *instructional development,* and (c) *organizational development* (POD Network, 2011b). While the specific uses of these terms often overlap, they share a common goal: the development of the fullest potential of existing institutional resources and structures by viewing and using them in creative ways.

Individual development generally refers to those programs that focus on the instructor as a teacher. Development specialists provide consultation on teaching, including class organization, grading and evaluation of student learning, in-class presentation skills, facilitation of class discussion, and all aspects of design and presentation. They also advise faculty on other aspects of teacher/learner interaction, such as advising, tutoring, discipline, and administration.

In addition to focusing on the instructor as a teacher, individual development programs also focus on the instructor as a scholar, professional, and person. Programs focused on scholarly and professional development offer assistance in career planning and academic work such as grant writing, publishing, committee service, administration, supervision, and a wide range of other activities expected of instructors and academic professionals. Personal development programs focus on wellness management, interpersonal skills, stress and time management, assertiveness, work-life balance, and a host of other issues related to individual well-being. While not all individual development programs include all these areas, most of them have as their philosophy the instructor as the driving force behind the institution; therefore, assisting that person to be as productive as possible will make the entire institution more effective.

Instructional development usually takes a different approach toward improving educational experiences. These programs have as their focus the course, curriculum, teaching, and student learning. In this approach, instructors together with faculty developers become members of a design or redesign team, working to identify appropriate course structures and teaching strategies to achieve the goals of instruction. Instructional development training involves the presentation of workshops on course design, alternative instructional methods, materials production, and so on. It also frequently includes a research component, often called the scholarship of teaching and learning (SoTL), which either focuses on a variety of questions about instructional effectiveness or assists instructors in conducting their own studies of course teaching methods and/or student learning outcomes.

Some instructional development programs have expanded the traditional focus on faculty to include training part-time instructors and teaching assistants—individuals frequently called on to teach first-year seminars. Instructional development programs can also examine how a course fits into the overall departmental and institutional curriculum, define instructional goals and methods that will maximize learning, evaluate course effectiveness in terms of goal achievement, and produce or evaluate learning materials for use in the course. Many instructional development programs include a media design component.

Organizational development maximizes institutional effectiveness by focusing on the structure, as well as policies and procedures of the institution and its subcomponents. The underlying principle is that if one can build or revise organizational structures to be efficient and effective in supporting instructors, staff, and students, the teaching/learning process will naturally thrive.

An example of organizational development change is represented by the very existence of first-year seminars and programs to support successful academic transition from high school to higher education. The initiative to create such programs came from student affairs units together with campus administrative leaders and was at heart an organizational development change that facilitated improved student performance, learning, and retention.

Organizational development activities can also include workshops for academic department chairs, cocurricular and student affairs department directors, deans, and other decision makers. The reasoning is that these are the individuals who will be making the policies that affect the ways that (a) courses are taught; (b) faculty are hired and promoted; and (c) learners are admitted, supported, and graduated. If those policies allow for growth and flexibility while maintaining standards, the amount of learning that occurs will increase.

The Faculty Development Learning Cycle

A five-step process modified from Groccia and Fink (2008) for teaching improvement is represented in Figure 1.3 below. Step 1 involves opportunities to learn about teaching methods and ideas through the study of books, articles, and other literature; participation in workshops, seminars, and classes; and information-sharing among colleagues and developers. The second step in this learning cycle is the application or use of such information. Instructors try out new approaches in a reflective way that collects data for future assessment (step 3). Learning outcomes data as well as teaching evaluation feedback from learners, self, and colleagues are collected and analyzed. These data are then shared with colleagues or an instructional development consultant for their feedback and suggestions (step 4). Learners can also be included in this sharing process as they often provide a valuable perspective on interpreting the assessment data. Step 5 involves further instructor reflection on what went well and what needs to be changed or modified. The result of this reflection is additional learning: The faculty member teaches in a way that incorporates what was learned and repeats the cycle. The faculty development learning cycle guides the discussion of instructor training and development in chapters 2 through 6 in this volume.

Research supports the need for a faculty development model that includes instruction, opportunity for practice, and feedback. For example, Skeff (n.d.) reported on a 1983 study evaluating an approach to improving the teaching performance of attending physicians called the Intensive Feedback Method in which instructors were videotaped and received feedback on their teaching from their students and house staff. They then worked with an educational consultant on teaching and completed teaching self-assessments. These instructors were then compared with those who had no intervention. Skeff found that 40% of the instructors improved by the end of the program, as judged by a blind rating system. Of those who received no intervention, only 1 of 16 improved, even on issues that they had identified as priorities for improvement.

Skeff came to two simple but powerful conclusions that support the need for faculty and instructor development: Teaching (a) will not improve on its own and (b) may deteriorate without intervention.

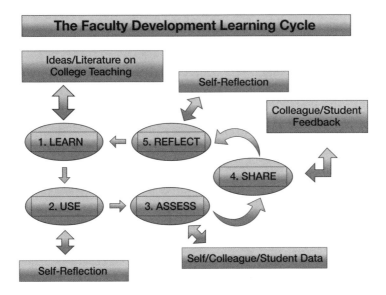

Figure 1.3. The faculty development learning cycle. Adapted from "Faculty Development and Institutional Quality: Creating the Link," by J. E. Groccia and L. D. Fink, 2008, Presentation at the 2008 International Consortium for Educational Development Conference, Salt Lake City, UT.

Conclusion

Higher education, beginning with first-year courses, will play a central role in the meeting the needs of learners and societies embedded in new world economic, political, and social realities. Faculty members and all educators teaching first-year seminars need to be trained and supported in creating engaged learning experiences that facilitate attainment of the new learning outcomes suggested by AAC&U and other educational experts. Active, collaborative, and cross-disciplinary teaching approaches are critical for first-year success and persistence, and instructors need to be provided opportunities to learn and apply these methods. Well-designed and cultivated faculty and instructor development programs for first-year seminar instructors are a perfect place for these efforts to begin.

Chapter 2
Organizing for Success

The strategic design and development of training programs for first-year seminar instructors is a critical factor in their success. Training efforts should be planned and delivered with existing elements of campus culture in mind. What works on one campus many not automatically work on another campus. For example, the length of training varies tremendously. Respondents to the 2009 National Survey of First-Year Seminars (Padgett & Keup, 2011) most commonly reported training programs of a half day or less (36.7%), followed by one-day events (21.7%), two-day events (11.5%), three-day events (5.1%), one week (3.1%), and training lasting four days (1.2%). The remaining 20.7% reported some other format and duration for their training program, which included ongoing training and development efforts and, in some cases, one-on-one mentoring.

Even though the initial exposure instructors have to faculty development is critically important, the authors view training for instructors of first-year seminars as extending beyond one-time workshops and strongly recommend the development of more long-term training programs that provide continuous professional development over an extended period of time. An extended training program exposes instructors to a broader and richer range of topics and perspectives enabling them to provide the best quality teaching to first-year learners.

Figure 2.1 presents an 11-step approach for planning, developing, and delivering a variety of training events—from continuous faculty development initiatives to one-shot programs—in higher education settings. The first four steps constitute a task analysis to guide the design and delivery of useful training procedures and material. The last six steps constitute the design and development process. Reference to the 11 steps, as well as additional suggestions concerning them, is found throughout this volume. For example, step 1 is addressed in chapter 6. Ideas that support steps 2 through 7 can be found throughout chapters 3 and 4. Discussion of steps 5, 6, and 10, which focus on the design and implementation of training activities, are the primary focus of this chapter. This chapter opens with suggestions for designing a comprehensive instructor development program for first-year seminars, offering an institutional example. The chapter also describes the design and delivery of individual training events. Steps 8, 9, and 11 involve ongoing evaluation and assessment of training efforts, which is addressed at the end of this chapter.

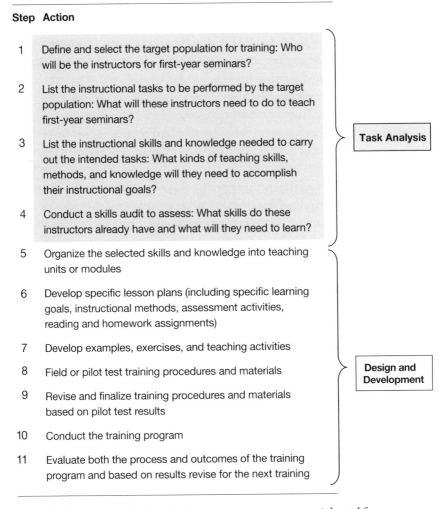

Step	Action	
1	Define and select the target population for training: Who will be the instructors for first-year seminars?	
2	List the instructional tasks to be performed by the target population: What will these instructors need to do to teach first-year seminars?	
3	List the instructional skills and knowledge needed to carry out the intended tasks: What kinds of teaching skills, methods, and knowledge will they need to accomplish their instructional goals?	Task Analysis
4	Conduct a skills audit to assess: What skills do these instructors already have and what will they need to learn?	
5	Organize the selected skills and knowledge into teaching units or modules	
6	Develop specific lesson plans (including specific learning goals, instructional methods, assessment activities, reading and homework assignments)	
7	Develop examples, exercises, and teaching activities	
8	Field or pilot test training procedures and materials	Design and Development
9	Revise and finalize training procedures and materials based on pilot test results	
10	Conduct the training program	
11	Evaluate both the process and outcomes of the training program and based on results revise for the next training	

Figure 2.1. Designing a faculty development training program. Adapted from "The 10-Step Process for Developing Training Courses," by the World Health Organization, 1998.

A Comprehensive Approach to Instructor Training and Development

A review of the kinds of faculty development training provided in U.S. universities highlights the variety of approaches that can be used in training programs. These formats have been by grouped by Sorcinelli, Austin, Eddy, and Beach (2006) into the following categories: (a) consultations for individual instructors, (b) institution-wide orientations, (c) institution-wide workshops, (d) intensive programs, (e) grants and awards for individuals and departments, (f) resources and publications, and (g) other services. Each of these approaches is appropriate for instructors teaching first-year seminars and can become an important component in a comprehensive model of instructor training.

Consultations for individual instructors may consist of a number of phases often in a somewhat sequential order. Consultation usually begins with a discussion and clarification of instructional goals and objectives. This groundwork and understanding process is critical but can be overlooked as the need for immediate improvement is often such that change is initiated without clear understanding of desired outcomes. From this foundation, data from the assessment of current teaching practices including the review of seminar materials, formal learner feedback (e.g., mid- or end-of-semester student ratings data), informal learner comments, class observation, or videotaping, are reviewed. With these data in hand different teaching strategies can be suggested and an action plan for change instituted. The consultative process continues as the instructor implements change and reviews learner behavior and learning results. Based on these outcomes, additional recommendations can be offered and implemented and their impact assessed. Consultations can be done by the first-year program leader, by the seminar director, or though collaboration with the institution's center for teaching and learning.

Institution-wide orientations and workshops. Many campus-wide faculty development units offer orientation programs for new faculty, graduate teaching assistants, and to a lesser degree, part-time instructors. Specially designed orientation programs for new first-year seminar instructors can be integrated into general campus wide orientations or conducted as stand-alone programs. University-wide workshops and seminars are standard aspects of faculty development programs using professional faculty developers as well as capitalizing on the expertise of regular faculty and graduate students. Integrating instructors who demonstrate expertise in teaching first-year learners into these workshops provides relevance and a direct connection to successful practice.

Intensive trainings. Training for first-year seminar instructors can also occur through intensive training programs and seminars that can range from one or two days to weeklong institutes to semester or yearlong faculty learning communities. Such intensive ongoing programs can combine a wide array of activities including individual consultation, orientations, workshops and seminars, mentoring, book or reading clubs, and a final teaching development project.

Grants and awards. First-year programs can, if funding sources exist, offer grants and awards to individual instructors or the departments from which these instructors are drawn. Grants can provide funding for course or curriculum development and design, attendance at conferences or workshops to explore new instructional approaches, or to present findings from the investigation of new seminar teaching techniques.

Resources and publications. Central to most faculty development programs is access to information, resources, and publications. This is done through a combination of print, multimedia (e.g., videotapes, DVDs, CD-ROMs, PODcasts), and electronic media. Websites have become a staple of faculty development programs and provide the added advantage of being able to link to resources from other first-year experience and faculty development programs and higher education entities.

Supporting and Sustaining Innovative Teaching Through Ongoing Development Opportunities

A critical factor in the success of first-year seminar instructor training programs is the ability of the seminar program to support and sustain the new teaching strategies learned during the training. If the new approaches to teaching and learning are not sustainable over time or if faculty who are implementing these new approaches are not supported so that teaching innovations can be continued, the effectiveness of such training can be seriously questioned. A landmark study prepared for the U.S. Office of Education in 1973 sheds light on the success of implementing and sustaining innovations of federal programs supporting educational change (Berman & McLaughlin, 1978). The authors found that effective strategies to sustain and support teaching innovation promoted mutual adaptation (i.e., the project was adapted to the reality of its institutional setting and teachers and school officials adapted their practices to the requirements and scope of the project). Effective support strategies also provided each instructor with necessary and timely feedback, allowed project-level choices to be made to correct problems, and encouraged commitment to the project. While this multi-year study focused on federally funded programs designed to develop and spread innovative teaching practices in public schools, application to first-year seminar instructional innovations seems appropriate. Specific recommendations include:

» *Providing extended seminar-specific instructor training.* Training programs need to be sensitive to each instructor's needs and abilities and should not be one-shot efforts. Follow-up sessions, either individual or group, need to be provided to administer training booster shots to keep up the motivation and levels of enthusiasm. Such follow-up sessions might include suggested strategies for teaching especially challenging course topics and learning outcomes (e.g., diversity, sexual health and wellness, emotional intelligence constructs, current issues on campus) or new ideas for building a community of scholars in the classroom.

» *Providing ongoing support and assistance from the first-year program administration.* The connection between individual instructors and the seminar administrators should be maintained over time. This can be done through meetings; refresher training sessions; personal contact; or through the implementation of e-mail, websites, or social networking media. Training and seminar instructor alumni should be kept together through reunions or other longitudinal support mechanisms to provide continued recognition and connection to seminar and institutional leadership. Additional suggestions for engaging instructors in continuous development are addressed in chapter 6.

» *Distributing regular print or electronic newsletters and updates to newly trained as well as seasoned seminar instructors.* These newsletters can contain information about program and institution policies and procedures; feature the accomplishments of seminar instructors and first-year students; highlight national news and information about first-year programs; contain news about local, national, and international conferences and workshops as well as grant funding opportunities; and provide listings of additional material and information to enhance instructor success.

» *Providing opportunities for seminar instructors to observe other instructors at their institution.* In addition to providing feedback to the instructor being observed, peer observation allows the observer to feel part of a larger community of others engaged in comparative learning activities and to witness other instructional approaches. Seeing others doing what one is also doing helps dissipate the sense that one is alone in this different educational venture and helps spread the feeling that one is instead a part of a larger effort being pursued by other respected professionals.

» *Encouraging seminar instructors to engage in national/international networks of higher educators sharing their interests related to first-year seminars* via listservs, conference attendance, and other professional development opportunities beyond their own campus setting. Opportunities for instructors to observe or visit (either electronically or face-to-face) similar programs at other institutions may also be considered.

» *Scheduling regular meetings for seminar instructors.* Regular meetings to discuss the practical issues and problems that arise can support new teaching practices. It is important for instructors to be able to share what is working and, conversely, what is not working with other instructors. Not only does this provide workable solutions, but it also builds trust and respect for others, factors that support maintaining innovation.

» *Establishing an instructional resource library either within the first-year seminar office or within the campus-wide center for teaching and learning.* Books and articles about first-year seminars, first-year programs, and teaching and learning can be cataloged and made accessible to instructors.

» *Adapting training and seminar materials to fit local needs and circumstances.* While the materials developed by others, including the National Resource Center, may be of exceptionally high quality, those that are modified and tailored to local realities will carry more importance and will be perceived as more relevant to one's training and seminar participants and first-year program. It is easier to sustain what we see as ours rather than what we think has been developed for different kinds of learners at various institutions.

» *Involving senior institutional and seminar administrators in the training program.* Ensure that key academic and student affairs administrators make their presence known and participate in the training. When instructors perceive that the seminar program is important enough for such leaders to take the time to be involved, the value of their work is reinforced. When senior institutional and seminar administrators view instructors' work as important, instructors are more likely to persevere in difficult times with the knowledge that the seminar matters to powerful others.

A Comprehensive Faculty Development Model: University 101

The Annual Professional Development Plan for the first-year seminar (University 101 Programs) at the University of South Carolina illustrates a comprehensive approach to ongoing instructor development (Figure 2.2). Four events—syllabus preparation workshops, an annual conference, a summer workshop series, and fall faculty meetings—comprise an annual cycle of training opportunities. The entry point, the Teaching Experience Workshop, is set outside the annual cycle of events because individuals attend this workshop only once. The three-day interactive and active-learning workshop is prerequisite to selection as an instructor. Considered a basic training, the workshop content includes:

» History, philosophy, and success of the seminar program
» Information on today's college students
» Goals, content, and learning outcomes of the first-year seminar
» Principles and pedagogies of effective teaching (i.e., fostering student learning, teaching and learning theory)
» Assessment of student learning
» Strategies for developing effective lesson plans and assignments for major content components of University 101
» Fundamentals of grading student work and effective feedback strategies
» Community development strategies
» Resource development
» Syllabus development

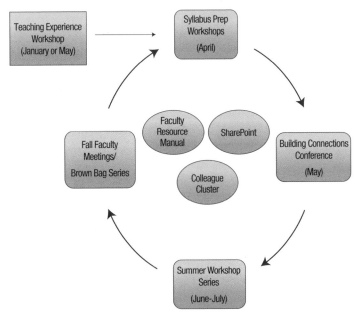

Figure 2.2. University 101 Programs annual professional development plan.

All instructors scheduled to teach in the following academic year attend two annual events. All teaching teams (i.e., instructor with peer or graduate leader) participate in a Syllabus Preparation Workshop, a 90-minute event that includes a review of the program assessment results from the previous year, the components of effective syllabi, discussions of the roles of each member of the teaching team, and other program updates. The day-long Building Connections Conference is an on-campus event for all seminar faculty and staff instructors and includes a keynote or panel presentation, topical concurrent sessions, a luncheon where the annual awards for outstanding teaching are presented, and a resource fair where campus partners provide information on programs and services that support the course learning outcomes and student success. Content for the conference is based on the results of the course evaluations and assessment results from the previous fall semester and/ or current campus needs and initiatives that impact the seminar. Continuous improvement is the guiding principle.

The Summer Workshop Series, scheduled throughout the summer months, offer repeat presentations of the concurrent sessions from the Building Connections Conference, providing opportunities for instructors to participate in sessions they were unable to attend at the conference. During the fall semester, several optional faculty meetings are held where instructors bring a brown bag lunch and hear program updates, share ideas with one another, clarify emerging issues, and enjoy community building activities. University 101 Programs also sponsors a Brown Bag Series, small-group meetings designed to provide support for special populations of instructors (e.g., first-time instructors, instructors of specific types of course sections). These informal gatherings allow instructors to share best practices and seek assistance as needed.

Three additional resources are available for instructors throughout the year. The *Faculty Resource Manual* is a 500-page binder with resources to support many aspects of teaching in general and the first-year seminar in particular (i.e., resources and strategies to address the 13 learning outcomes of the course). SharePoint is an intranet software that provides a forum for discussion, a place to share resources, and a mechanism for distributing information. Instructors can access electronic course materials, such as videos, PowerPoint presentations, and an electronic version of the *Faculty Resource Manual* so that they can customize activities and handouts. Other features of this site include a discussion board for sharing ideas and a comprehensive calendar, with important dates for the course (e.g., faculty meetings, workshops), academic calendar (e.g., drop/add, semester breaks), and institution-wide events (e.g., involvement fair). Finally, all instructors are invited to join a colleague cluster. These clusters of five to six diverse instructors meet periodically over coffee or lunch to share ideas as communities of practice (Wenger, 1998), learn from one another, and support each other's professional development and teaching.

The Design and Delivery of Individual Training Events

While the most effective instructor training models for first-year seminars will involve ongoing support and development opportunities, the entry into the teaching corps for the seminar is frequently a single training event. In other cases, institutions may offer an annual training experience for both new and returning instructors. Gardner (1981, 1992) presents a model for first-year seminar instructor training events that has been used at the University of South Carolina and widely replicated at other institutions. The model is based on four phases, which both guide the process and inform the content of training events (Figure 2.3). It is adaptable and can be used to design training regardless of seminar type, learning objectives, and content.

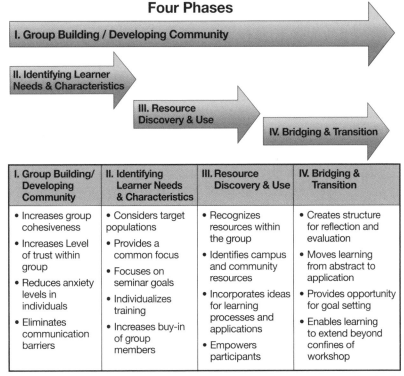

Four Phases

I. Group Building/ Developing Community	II. Identifying Learner Needs & Characteristics	III. Resource Discovery & Use	IV. Bridging & Transition
• Increases group cohesiveness	• Considers target populations	• Recognizes resources within the group	• Creates structure for reflection and evaluation
• Increases Level of trust within group	• Provides a common focus	• Identifies campus and community resources	• Moves learning from abstract to application
• Reduces anxiety levels in individuals	• Focuses on seminar goals	• Incorporates ideas for learning processes and applications	• Provides opportunity for goal setting
• Eliminates communication barriers	• Individualizes training	• Empowers participants	• Enables learning to extend beyond confines of workshop
	• Increases buy-in of group members		

Figure 2.3. Four-Phase Model: An adaptable model for first-year seminar faculty development. Adapted from "Developing Faculty as Facilitators and Mentors" by J. N. Gardner, 1981, *New Directions for Student Services*, 14, pp. 67-80. Copyright 1981 by Jossey-Bass; and from *Freshman Seminar Instructor Training: Guidelines for Design and Implementation* by J. N. Gardner, Copyright 1992 by University of South Carolina.

As the arrows illustrate, the workshop/event begins with a group-building phase that continues to develop throughout the life of the group. After a solid foundation is formed among workshop participants and facilitators, the workshop continues with a focus on the needs of the learners (first-year students) and then logically moves into a phase of identifying resources to meet learner needs. The event concludes with attention to bridging and transition in which participants are guided in considering how what has been learned in the workshop can be applied in the first-year seminar, and perhaps other, settings.

The Syllabus as an Organizing Frame

Many of the same principles underlying the planning and delivery of courses for students apply to those designing faculty development experiences. The syllabus is the coin of the realm for outlining learning experiences (e.g., courses) in colleges and universities. Each time they teach, instructors organize their course, communicate their expectations, and outline important aspects for students in the syllabus. The syllabus can also be a useful strategy for planning and organizing faculty development events. Figure 2.4 outlines the contents of a syllabus for faculty development. Using the syllabus outline for planning purposes will help designers consider the variety of aspects necessary to organize a meaningful and productive experience for participants. Appendix A provides a sample syllabus for a three-day instructor development workshop offered at the University of South Carolina.

Syllabus for a Faculty Development Event

Goal Statement

Expectations

Learning Outcomes for Participants

Tools, Texts, Materials, and Resources Needed

Requirements of Participants

     Prerequisites

     Preparation

     Attendance

     Participation

Facilitators' Content Outline /Agenda

Assessment

Future Development and Ongoing Needs

Notes

Figure 2.4. Syllabus for a faculty development event.

Elements of Successful Instructor Training Events

While content and process of training events are of critical importance, logistical considerations also contribute to the quality and success of instructor development efforts. Hunter and Cuseo (1999) provide useful suggestions for elements to consider when developing an initial seminar instructor training program.

» *Place.* The training site should be comfortable and inviting; accessible both in terms of distance from campus (or instructors' work areas on campus) and in terms of ease of ingress and egress for those with mobility impairments; well equipped with the latest technology; of appropriate size to accommodate all participants without crowding; furnished with tables, desks, and chairs that enable movement and active learning experiences; and offer minimal distractions. While Gardner (1992) suggests that an off-campus retreat center location is ideal, this is not always possible. Therefore, efforts to create a place that mimics a retreat center ambiance while in an on-campus location should be what trainers strive to achieve.

» *Quality.* As Hunter and Cuseo recommend, plan the event with class! The food, drink, printed material, and handouts should be of the highest quality possible. First impressions are often lasting impressions, and what trainees see during the training will communicate messages about how the first-year program is run and its overall quality.

» *Institutional buy-in.* The seminar training program should communicate institutional buy-in and commitment. This can be done by including a high-level institutional leader to welcome participants or address them at some point during the event. This symbolic and structural action is an important marker of the importance and value of first-year programs.

» *Evidence.* An important element of first-year programs is to include some evidence of the impact and effectiveness of such programs. Local data, if available, as well as national data on how first-year seminars impact learners' lives, academic as well as social, should be shared with instructors.

» *Trainee input.* Training programs should provide participants the opportunity to have some choice or input in the program in terms of range or sequencing of topics to be covered as well as format and duration of the training. Frequently achieved through an evaluation process, attending to trainee input can help continuously improve efforts.

» *Breaking the ice.* Training programs should begin with activities that encourage team building and meaningful rapport among participants and facilitators. Community building exercises provide a relaxed way to get to know fellow trainees and to help get past the awkward initial stages. Faculty members or instructors are at times hesitant and somewhat insecure when placed in situations where they are supposed to learn something new (especially information outside of one's discipline). Accustomed to being the expert in teaching and learning situations, faculty can be resistant to engaging in training or in assuming the role of novice learner. Icebreakers can help overcome that resistance and create a level playing field for all trainees.

» *Activity.* It cannot be reiterated enough that training sessions should avoid the use of passive methods of instruction as much as possible. While some information can be conveyed to participants through lecture, lectures should be short and interspersed with a wide variety of active-learning exercises that encourage trainee movement, discussion, problem solving, and critical thinking. Training should model the kind of teaching recommended in the first-year seminar.

» *Capitalizing on veteran instructors.* Whenever possible include veteran instructors in the training. Instructors who have taught first-year seminars can share their experiences with novice instructors. They have been in the trenches, so to speak, and what they say carries the authenticity and credibility of experience. Veteran instructors also serve as role models and can often be a source of future advice, as a new instructor might be more likely to seek the council of someone like them, rather than a first-year program administrator.

» *Relaxing and socializing.* Workshop planners should not shy away from building in time for relaxation and socializing. It is often during these down times that people form networks and interpersonal connections that can be vital to instructor satisfaction and success.

» *Culminating activity.* A well-planned, constructed, and delivered training event should end on a positive note. The workshop design should include some kind of closure activity or celebration of accomplishment where trainees are recognized and congratulated. A group photo brings people together in a way that is captured for posterity and serves as a symbol of entry and membership in the club of dedicated seminar instructors.

Strategies for Evaluating Training Efforts

Evaluation of faculty development initiatives is an important function of continuous improvement of such efforts. Three reasons for evaluating seminar instructor training and faculty development programs include (a) improving current and future programs, (b) determining whether a program should be continued, and (c) justifying the existence of the training program (Kirkpatrick & Kirkpatrick, 2006). In difficult fiscal times, the second and third reasons can overshadow the first. Assessments can be conducted, or judgments reached, about the effectiveness of faculty development efforts at five different points in the training process: before, during, and after faculty development training (prior to teaching in the seminar or classroom) as well as during or after teaching in the seminar or classroom (Kirkpatrick & Kirkpatrick). Figure 2.5 illustrates these times of evaluation.

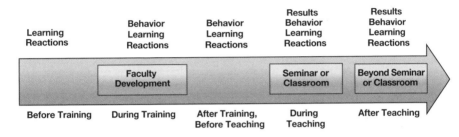

Figure 2.5. Five-point assessment model. Adapted from *Evaluating Training Programs* (3rd ed.) by D. L. Kirkpatrick and J. D. Kirkpatrick. Copyright 2006, Berrett-Kohler Publishers.

Participants, as well as the overall training program, can be assessed on four levels (Nickols, 2000), also represented in Figure 2.5. These levels include reactions, learning, behavior, and results, and are described in greater detail below.

» ***Reactions*** are defined by how well the trainees liked a particular program and are typically measured at the end of training (i.e., summative assessment). However, reactions can also be measured during the training (i.e., formative assessment). Such assessments might be formal (i.e., asking participants to respond to brief survey or prompt about the training program thus far) or informally in terms of the instructor's perceptions of participants' reactions. Trainee reactions assessed during the training can be cycled back and used to improve the immediate experience. Reactions to training can also be assessed prior to training to gauge instructor preferences and reactions to previous training programs, again to improve the current training experience.

» *Learning* indicates the degree to which principles, facts, and techniques were understood and absorbed by the participants. Evaluating learning can take place at all five points in the assessment process before, during, and after training.

» *Behavior* is the change in instructor or trainee behavior. Any evaluation of changes in teaching behavior must occur in the classroom or within the seminar situation itself. However, it can be useful to assess behavior changes at the end of training, in the classroom, and even beyond the seminar in future teaching ventures. The latter can be done through direct observation of teaching or by student ratings using classroom assessment techniques or end-of-semester student evaluations.

» *Results* are the actual changes in seminar student learning outcomes. Student behavior, attitudes, or values that change as a result of the faculty development or seminar instructor training may be the most meaningful measure of effectiveness. In many cases, however, they may be the most difficult to assess. These factors are measurable in the classroom as scores on exams or other assignments or at some time after the classroom experience in the student's subsequent classes or in his or her work performance.

According to McNamara (2010), movement further down in these levels indicates a more valid and useful evaluation. In other words, measuring the results or effectiveness of a training program is a more accurate assessment of impact than simply measuring the trainee's personal reactions or learning.

Conclusion

Faculty development training programs for first-year seminar instructors will benefit from a strategic and comprehensive process of planning and implementation. This chapter presented a step-by-step approach for strategic planning and carrying out training programs, offered an institutional example of a comprehensive model, described elements of successful training events, provided suggestions for ongoing or continuous instructor development, and addressed the evaluation of training efforts.

Chapter 3
Applying Theory and Research About Learning to Instructor Training and First-Year Seminars

This chapter will focus on preparing instructors to teach first-year seminars. There is no *right* way to design and deliver training for first-year seminar instructors. The format and content that these training sessions take will depend on many variables such as institutional context and traditions, trainer expertise and experience, goals of the training program, level of teaching preparation and experience of the seminar instructors, available funding, and the timing of the training program. The scope and size of training programs will also depend on the number of students engaged in first-year seminars and the corresponding number of instructors needed; levels of institutional support available; placement of seminar courses within the academic or student affairs structures; integration of seminar courses with departmental, unit, or institutional strategic plans; alignment of seminar courses with institutional retention efforts; course funding mechanisms; and institutional policies and procedures. There is also variability in the content of instructor training for many of the same reasons. Issues related to content will be addressed in chapter 4.

The authors suggest, however, that planning efforts for effective instructor training should consider two very important components: (a) general theories of learning and (b) theories of adult learning, in particular, so that this knowledge can be applied to training efforts. Providing workshops, courses, and other training activities for faculty and other instructors of first-year seminars will be most effective if faculty developers consider how adult learners may differ from children and adolescents. Thus, the first part of this chapter provides a brief overview of adult learning principles to guide these efforts and then summarizes theories and research on how people learn in general.

Theories of Adult Learning

Faculty developers should be guided by an understanding of adult development and lifelong learning principles. Andragogy, a set of core learning principles that apply to all adult learning situations initially developed by Malcolm Knowles (Knowles, Holton, & Swanson, 2005), is a useful framework for creating and offering activities for adults (faculty and staff) to enhance teaching and learning for first-year students. The andragogical, adult learning model differs greatly from the traditional pedagogical model that has guided education and is based on the following six assumptions:

1. *Learner's need to know.* Adults need to know the purpose for what they are learning and what they will be expected to do before the learning activity takes place. Learning outcomes need to be clearly stated and the reasons for instructional methods used should be described at the onset of each instructional activity. The first task of the developer is to ensure that participants in the training program understand the value and nature of what will be learned and the methods of teaching that will be employed. When this happens, adults are more likely to buy in to the learning experience and commit energy to attaining the desired learning outcomes.

2. *Learner's self-concept.* Adults typically have a greater sense of self-responsibility than younger people and many of the students they teach. As such, they need to be perceived as being capable and self-directed. Developers need to communicate a sense of self-efficacy so that participants see themselves not as dependent upon the developer but as being self-directed learners. Active-learning experiences that engage adults directly in creating meaning as well as self-directed activities where they assume greater levels of personal responsibility for their learning are very effective.

3. *Role of prior experience.* Adults bring a greater volume and variety of previous learning simply by virtue of having lived longer than the typical undergraduate. This often translates to a greater range of differences and heterogeneity in learning styles, motivation, behaviors, needs, values, interests, and goals. Instructors' prior experiences need to be integrated into faculty development activities in a way that channels this rich diversity toward the attainment of the developer's goals. At the same time, trainers need to be aware that participants may enter development experiences with a sense that they already know the information. Some adult learners are resistant to change, new ideas, or different ways of doing things. This is often played

out in faculty development workshops by statements such as "We tried that before and it didn't work" or "Here comes another educational fad that was tried before and failed." This kind of resistance can best be overcome by sharing the rationale and evidence in support of new teaching techniques and faculty development efforts.

4. *Readiness to learn.* Adults will learn things when they believe that new information will help them function effectively in the here and now. This suggests that a just-in-time approach to training may be especially effective with some learners.

5. *Orientation to learning.* Adults are life-, task-, or problem-centered in their orientation to learning. They are motivated to learn what they perceive to be useful to accomplish pragmatic real-world goals or address real-life situations. For developers, this means that the material needs to connect to instructor concerns, be couched in terms that instructors understand, and use examples and methods that reflect common issues in his or her discipline. Relevance is important in teaching first-year students today and is true for adults as well.

6. *Motivation to learn.* The most potent motivators of learning for adults relate to internal factors, what have been called intrinsic motivators (e.g., the desire to do a good job, self-esteem, the opportunity to learn new things). Developers need to capitalize on this internal motivation to learn and use extrinsic, or external rewards, judiciously. This can be difficult, however, in an academic environment that is pressure packed (especially for new, untenured faculty) and geared toward tangible outcomes and visible markers of success (e.g., tenure, promotion, the next grant proposal or published paper). First-year seminar instructors who come from student affairs, the library, or other sectors of the institution may find that balancing pressures of their primary role with first-year seminar responsibilities can be daunting and may obscure their initial motivation to participate in these programs. (Knowles et al.)

In sum, adult learners bring a set of expectations, experiences, and attitudes that influence their learning. An understanding of these will provide a sound theoretical basis from which to design effective training opportunities for those preparing instructors to teach first-year seminars. In addition, these adult learning principles should be communicated to first-year instructors to assist with their own design of learning experiences for their students.

Theories and Research on Learning

Bransford, Brown, and Cocking (2000) suggest that knowing how people learn may help faculty choose among a variety of techniques to accomplish specific learning goals. Those preparing instructors to teach first-year students also need to do so with a sound understanding of both theories and research on how people learn, especially college students. Additionally, this information should be communicated directly to first-year seminar instructors to provide a theoretical and empirical basis for designing effective learning opportunities. Learning experiences in training can serve as models for designing learning experiences in the seminar. As such, much of what is outlined in this chapter applies to both the instructor development experience and the first-year seminar. Thus, the terms *developers, trainers, instructors,* and *designers* will be used throughout the chapter to indicate individuals leading faculty development activities and those teaching first-year seminars. The following points summarize what faculty developers should know to enhance their work with first-year instructors who, in turn, must use the information to develop and instruct effective first-year seminars.

1. Information has to be processed and practiced to be learned.

Psychologists and educators look toward computer models to understand and enhance human learning. Groccia's (1992) Information Processing Model of Learning (Figure 3.1), based on Atkinson and Shiffrin's (1968) multi-store model of memory, depicts the processes in which humans attend to, store, process, and retrieve information. Information is processed and stored in stages: (a) attending to the stimulus, (b) recognizing its importance, (c) transforming it into some type of mental symbol, (d) comparing it with already stored information to assess its meaningfulness, and (e) then acting on it in some way (Searleman & Herrmann, 1994). When this is done, information is stored in short-term memory and, if processed further through encoding (input and study) and decoding (retrieval, output, and practice) strategies, it gets stored into long-term memory.

Human memory is both limited and limitless (Snowman, McCown, & Biehler, 2009). Our sense organs (sensory register) have a limited ability to respond to environmental stimuli and store information about the world in a fairly unprocessed way for about one to three seconds. In the sensory register, information that is not actively attended to will disappear from memory. When information is recognized and attended to in the sensory register, it

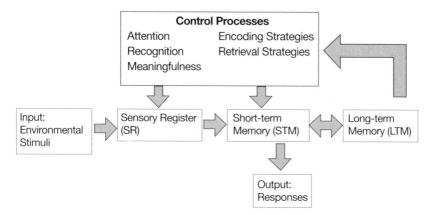

Figure 3.1. Information processing model of learning. Adapted from *The College Success Book: A Whole-Student Approach to Academic Excellence* by J. E. Groccia, 1992, p. 110. Copyright 1992 by Glenbridge Publishing. Reprinted with permission.

will be processed and transferred to short-term memory. Short-term memory is just that, with limits on how much information can be stored (approximately seven unrelated items) and for how long (approximately 10 to 20 seconds). However, once stored in long-term memory, the absolute amount of information retained and learned appears to be limitless.

The control processes indicated in Figure 3.1 are those actions that the learner performs to facilitate long-term memory storage. The control processes help determine the quantity and quality of information that the learner stores and retrieves from memory (Snowman et al., 2009). The learner determines when and where to use these processes; and he or she directly, actively, and consciously manipulates them. The following suggestions are useful for developing programs and workshops to train first-year seminar instructors and for designing seminar activities that help students become effective information processors and learners (Snowman et al.).

Develop and use a variety of teaching techniques to attract and hold attention. The faculty developer should use sudden, abrupt changes to the environment, print key words on the board, use well-designed PowerPoint presentations, provide verbal cues such as "This is an important point, take notice" or "You might want to write down what I am about to say" or the one that never fails for students, "This may be on the test." Starting class or the training session with some unexpected remarks, an interesting and related item recently reported in the news, or a dilemma or controversial issue related to the topic at hand can pique attention and get learners focused for mental processing (i.e., learning).

Learn what captures participants' attention. This can be facilitated by getting to know who your learners are. Collecting information about what they find interesting or meaningful, their goals and expectations for the training or course, or their hobbies or activities outside of work and class can provide suggestions for topics that may gain learners' attention.

To hold attention throughout the teaching experience, relate current experience with what learner will be doing in the future. Making connections between what the participants are learning in the training sessions and how this will be relevant in their teaching, classroom activities, or future educational experiences can deepen learning. Developers should use examples during the training or teaching that directly relate their natural interests and/or to what the facilitator or learner will experience in the seminar classroom.

Help learners recognize that what is being learned relates to what is already known. Recognition is an important control process that assists in learning, and trainers and facilitators need to help learners become better recognizers of important information. Facilitators should be direct and strategic, saying things such as, "In this session we will highlight the importance of engagement in learning. Does anyone recognize something familiar about this topic?" or "In this workshop, the same basic point will be made a number of ways. As you read and listen, try to recognize and write down the many different ways this point is made." Periodically have participants summarize key points in the workshop in their own words, or use a think-pair-share or one-minute paper approach where they are asked to write a few sentences summarizing the most important points and muddiest points needing additional clarification.

Encourage the use of spaced practice rather than massed practice. The material to be learned should be spread over multiple days or sessions rather than asking participants to learn everything all at once. For example, in a faculty development setting, rather that attempting to learn and understand a complete set of course outcomes, participants can focus on a few at a time. Most student learners, and many adult learners, are not only unaware of the benefits of distributed practice, but they go to great lengths to block off or mass study time into large uninterrupted sessions (Bjork, 1979). If modeled in instructor development and intentionally discussed, instructors are more likely to apply this concept to their teaching in the first-year seminar.

Use rehearsal techniques to enhance learning by breaking tasks into smaller, more manageable pieces. This can be done by having learners develop categories into which information can be placed. Placing or chunking items into groups reduces the number of pieces to be learned. Organizing information with outlines or mind maps facilitates encoding (i.e., learning) and provides additional cues for decoding (performing). When presenting information in training, faculty developers should provide an outline on the board, on an overhead projector, or in PowerPoint and encourage participants to take note under the various headings. Not only does this help learners take better and more complete notes, but it will also help highlight the sequence and relatedness of information covered. When presenting material to workshop participants or to seminar students, instead of teaching for large periods of time, the trainer should divide the material into a series of smaller lessons. Facilitators should stop every 15 to 20 minutes and introduce an activity, ask someone to summarize what was just presented, pose a question for discussion, or have the participants stand up. This will refocus attention and help chunk information into smaller more manageable and learner-friendly units.

Present material in concrete, visual ways. According to Paivio's (1986) dual-coding theory, the use of illustrations and tangible examples leads to higher level learning by increasing the meaningfulness and allowing it to be encoded into long-term memory in both visual and verbal formats (as cited in Snowman et al., 2009). Learners who are provided graphic organizers (e.g., mind or cognitive maps, illustrations, diagrams, outlines) are better able to learn information than those who are just provided verbal or textual material (Vekiri, 2002).

Put action before theory. Learners are often presented with an elaborate lecture on theory or background information and are then asked to work the example or solve a problem at home on their own. What often happens is that the learner struggles to apply the theory or solve the problem because he or she has nothing tangible to relate to the lecture content. Effective teachers rely on Kolb's (1981) *concrete experience* method of acquiring information instead. They begin the training session or class with an experiment or activity that engages learners in thinking about and performing a task relevant to the topic at hand. Participants can then be asked to reflect on or process the experience prior to being presented the theory behind the activity. Finally, participants can be asked to do something or actively experiment with what they have learned as a way to deepen the processing of new ideas. In this way, the activity provides a frame into which theory can be hung. Teaching abstract concepts in this way deepens learning and allows the learner to more easily move from theory to application.

Encourage active learning. Participants in faculty training and students in first-year seminars must do more than listen to learn. They must read, write, discuss, solve problems, and engage in activities that question and prod through higher-order thinking tasks involving analysis, synthesis, evaluation, and creation (see Bonwell & Eison, 1991). Research supports active approaches as an effective way to facilitate learning, and learners are more likely to internalize, understand, and remember material through active engagement in learning activities (Bonwell & Southerland, 1996). Silberman (1996) in his aptly named book, *Active Learning: 101 Strategies to Teach Any Subject*, provides tangible examples of active-learning techniques that can be integrated into both faculty training programs and first-year seminars.

2. Learning is a community endeavor.

Individuals often hold an image of a solitary scholar who sits alone quietly and learns without assistance from others. This is evidenced by the giving of credit to a single person for an invention, idea, or article, and by the common practice at universities of placing higher value on individual versus collaborative scholarship. Others conceptualize learning as the transfer of knowledge—the instructor as the source, the packaging agent, and the transporter of that knowledge and the learner as the receiver, or the passive empty vessel, for that knowledge.

Yet, learning is a social endeavor and good teaching encourages social, cooperative, interactive work that is not competitive and isolated. Two of Chickering and Gamson's (1987) seven principles for good practice in undergraduate education emphasize the importance of the social dimension to learning: (a) contact between learners and faculty and (b) reciprocity and cooperation among learners. Working together with others increases the involvement in learning. Faculty developers and instructors need to capitalize on the social nature of humans, on their need for belonging (Maslow, 1999), and create learning opportunities that use diads, triads, and larger groups of learners working together to answer questions, solve problems, and analyze and synthesize information.

In applying this concept to faculty development efforts, organizers should develop and use interactive learning techniques such as cooperative learning, small-group discussion, team-based learning, jigsaw, and so on (see Silberman, 1996). Trainers should structure the workshop or classroom situation so that participants are encouraged to work together freely. One should design the workshop or classroom so that every 15 to 20 minutes participants are engaged in answering questions, solving problems, or discussing readings together. Such active engagement on the part of the learner will keep them focused and involved in the learning experience.

It is important that trainers understand and use group dynamics principles in the workshop or classroom. Having learners work together can be fraught with problems. People with different ideas, ways of learning, and motivation levels do not always work together harmoniously or productively. Group work often fails, not because of its inherent pedagogical flaws, as some instructors and learners believe, but rather because of the human interaction dynamics involved when people work together (Miller, Wilkes, & Cheetham, 1993).

Tuckman (1965) developed a five-stage model of group performance that indicates that the effectiveness of groups is not immediate. He labeled these stages forming, storming, norming, performing, and adjourning. Each stage builds upon the preceding stage, and the effectiveness of group functioning requires that the instructor or workshop facilitator, as well as group participants, understand that this process is natural and normal. Additionally, all involved will benefit from knowing that the stages need to be worked through, that there will be conflict and discomfort in the process, but that these conflicts often lead to increased group effectiveness and productivity.

» *Forming.* The group comes together and gets to know each other. The group begins to experience a feeling of excitement, anticipation, and often, some doubt and concern. Reasons for the group to come together are discussed and the task is identified. Individuals begin to identify where they can fit within the group and how their talents can be best used.

» *Storming.* Members begin vying for position within the group. Conflict about leadership and task distribution, as well as group logistics (i.e., meeting times, due dates), often arise. Some group members respond with negativity, anxiety, and dissatisfaction as differences begin to surface.

» *Norming.* Eventually agreement is reached on how to proceed, who is to do what, what information is needed, and when tasks need to be finished. Group members establish cohesion around shared goals, acceptance of group member diversity and different ways of knowing and thinking, bond as team members, trust each other, and understand the need to work together.

» *Performing.* The group finally focuses on getting things finished and becomes effective in accomplishing its goals and objectives.

» *Adjourning.* Groups often experience reluctance to disband as they approach task completion. Negativity and difficulties that were previously resolved can resurface as a manifestation of not wanting to let go and move on. Crises can arise that delay group termination and prolong the group process.

These kinds of issues usually develop in longer-term learning groups and learners working together in workshops or class in short-term groups will probably not experience them to the degree described by Tuckman. Yet, Miller et al. (1993) have demonstrated that interpersonal conflict within groups will develop when people with different perspectives, experiences, values, and thinking and learning styles are mixed together. Trainers need to understand and anticipate some degree of conflict if group-learning activities are used. Similarly, instructors using group-learning methods in seminar courses also need to prepare for the potential of interpersonal conflict, and they should inform their students of this possibility.

Though some conflict is inevitable, faculty developers can employ a number of strategies to minimize it and develop community among an instructor corps. The following are examples of such strategies.

Establish learning communities. It can be helpful in training programs, especially those that are multi-day or multi-session to group participants into communities of learners who share common elements such as type of students or subjects taught. By doing so, the trainer provides support mechanisms that can reinforce content taught in the training. Studies have shown that learning communities can be effective in promoting academic achievement, academic and social integration, involvement, satisfaction, sense of community, and persistence among students (Avens & Zelley, 1992; Borden & Rooney, 1998; Buckner, 1977; Hill, 1985; Knight, n.d.; Lacy, 1978; Levine & Tompkins, 1996; Matthews, Smith, MacGregor, & Gabelnick, 1996; Schroeder & Hurst, 1996; Smith, 1991, 1993; Tinto, 1994; Tinto & Love, 1995; Tinto, Russo, & Kadel, 1994). Thus, it is possible that a similar strategy of developing learning communities among those involved in instructor development and first-year seminar instructor corps may achieve similar benefits.

Develop collaborative teaching relationships and peer-facilitated and supported teaching and learning. First-year seminar training programs need to engage participants as co-facilitators whenever possible. This is suggested for three reasons: (a) participants can learn from the experiences and perceptions of their peers, (b) learning is enhanced through the teaching process, and (c) the experience of peer instruction can model effective strategies for collaborative teaching in the seminar. For further reading on models and approaches to peer-facilitated and supported teaching approaches see Miller et al., (2001).

Establish learner/faculty mentoring programs. Instructors who participate in first-year seminar training programs will benefit from being paired or grouped with others who have participated in the past. Program directors can encourage first-year programs to capitalize on the expertise of successful instructors by developing mechanisms whereby they can mentor or consult with those currently in training or those who are in their first seminar instructional role. Likewise, instructors can bring students who have successfully completed the first-year seminar into the classroom to share their experiences with current students. Such efforts also help create a peer network that extends into the second or third academic year.

Create student/faculty interaction space. Both within the seminar training and the seminar experience itself, trainers and instructors should create some physical space where participants can share experiences and socialize. These informal spaces often cement collegial relationships and reinforce the learning that takes place in more formal instructional settings.

Involve learners in curricular development activities, academic committees, and organizations. Providing the learner, instructor and student alike, opportunities to participate in the design and selection of learning activities can enhance all instructional activities. One is more likely to engage in activities that he or she has had some responsibility in choosing than in those imposed by someone else. It is important for trainers to build in choice, be it in the sequence, timing, or content of the training activities. It is equally important for seminar instructors to provide opportunities for similar direct input from students.

First exposure to new material may be done alone, but for most people deep learning requires interaction and application with others (e.g., other learners and/or a instructor or facilitator). If seminar or training time allows, learners may get initial exposure to new material on their own (e.g., through reading, viewing a videotape) and then review and apply the material in time together with the instructor and/or other learners

3. Each person's learning process is different.

Individual difference has been a key concept in the psychology of learning since the earliest laboratory and classroom experiments. While we strive for principles that have general application to all learners, we must recognize human variety and diversity and provide opportunities for each learner to maximize his/her potential. Learners differ in experience, background, gender, age, physical and cognitive abilities, and learning styles. As noted earlier, this diversity often leads to increased group conflict but superior quality work (Miller et al., 1993). Students will take different approaches to learning based on the demands of the course and instructor, the learning context, and individual needs. Likewise, so will participants in faculty development experiences.

Since there will likely be a wide range of learning processes in any training group, faculty developers should use varied teaching approaches. Training sessions should combine learning activities that enable all participants to operate from a position of strength and comfort in terms of their preferred style. While trainers need not cater exclusively to participants' preferred learning styles, some attention should be placed on varying instruction so that different approaches (e.g., lecture, discussion, application) are integrated within each training segment. Accordingly, trainers should challenge and support learners to develop skill in and comfort with activities that focus on their non-preferred learning styles.

Similarly, training activities should use a range of sensory modalities (e.g., visual, auditory, tactile, movement). For example, PowerPoint presentations should include diagrams and charts and audio clips (e.g., music, spoken quotes, sounds) that reinforce the meaning of visual images in addition to text.

4. Emotions play a vital role in the learning process.

Western culture tends to downplay the importance of emotions. Science and school learning are portrayed as rational and logical. Emotions are portrayed as irrational and illogical and as being out of control. As such, emotions should be squelched, subdued, and controlled, especially during the learning process. Humanistic theory, as developed by Rogers (1961) and Maslow (1999), promoted humane education that considered the whole person (affect as well as intellect) in learning, but this theoretical approach was often criticized as unsupported by hard science. Yet, research in learning and brain functioning has supported the influence of emotions on learning (Ingleton, 1999; Sousa, 1995). For example, Sousa provides a useful description of brain processing, suggesting a hierarchy in how the brain responds to sensory input. Input and processing of material that is of higher priority diminishes the processing of lower-priority information. Highest priority is given to information that poses a threat to survival, such as a physical or emotional attack or lack of oxygen, and is processed immediately.

A first step in applying this element of learning is to understand and acknowledge the importance of emotion in the learning process. In the training setting, this means beginning the educational experience by creating and fostering a safe and welcoming learning environment. The use of ice-breakers or activities to assist participants with getting to know each other, sharing personal information, and rapport building is strongly recommended (e.g., Scannell & Newstrom, 1994).

Trainers and instructors communicate powerful messages, both verbally and nonverbally, that can influence participant and learner attitudes and behavior. Buskist, Sikorski, Buckley, and Saville (2002) and Schaeffer, Epting, Zinn, and Buskist (2003) in investigations of learner perceptions of effective teaching indicate that learners see the simple act of smiling as an important characteristic of an effective facilitator or instructor. Similarly, having realistic expectations, a good sense of humor, a positive outlook, and enthusiasm for teaching and being fair, knowledgeable about the topic, flexible and open-minded, understanding, approachable and personable, caring, respectful, creative, and interesting are among the 10 most important instructor characteristics according to students (Schaeffer et al.). All, with the exception of knowledgeable about topic, are personal characteristics that highlight the power of affective variables in effective teaching.

Highlighting academic rituals, ceremonies, and celebrations to acknowledge learner accomplishments can also serve to capitalize on the power of the emotional dimension of learning. Bringing positive attention to success fosters a sense of accomplishment and achievement, which can stimulate future motivation to learn. Providing each participant with a certificate (suitable for framing) is one tangible way to document and demonstrate to others successful completion of the training experience. Purkey and Novak (2008) discuss the power of providing positive invitations to learners by focusing on what they can achieve rather than their shortcomings. Over time, this invitational approach is internalized by learners and empowers them to succeed. Celebrations of accomplishment are powerful visual symbols of success that can help to reinforce these invitations.

Trainers can encourage the use of reflective journals and face-to-face, as well as online, discussions to allow participants to freely express emotions that can help them refine their thinking about previous actions, behaviors, and attitudes. Such writing often taps into affective as well as cognitive aspects of learning as participants are encouraged to make sense out of content or to filter this knowledge through personal experience.

5. The desire to make order and meaning is innate.

Humans have an innate need to make meaning out of chaos. People try to organize and simplify complex social, psychological, and physical realities with which they must cope on a day-to-day basis. Making meaning or formulating rules for what is experienced is real learning. Each learner has a unique "developmental niche" (Segall, Dasen, Berry, & Poortinga, 1990, p. 114) or cultural framework, which includes the physical and social contexts in which a child lives, culturally determined child-rearing and educational practices, and the psychological characteristics of one's parents. The cultural framework helps organize new information, but it also produces perceptual orientations that are resistant to change. In fact, survival and continued membership in the group requires maintaining these definitions or perceptions of how things work. As a result, these cultural realities can hinder future learning—especially classroom-based instruction.

When addressing the more deeply held mental models learners bring to the educational experience, the instructor or trainer might begin by finding out what learners believe they already know. A quiz or the use of clicker questions before a new topic is introduced is one way to achieve this. The quiz also serves as a good way to provide learners with a preview of what will subsequently be covered (i.e., a preview of coming attractions). Asking learners to describe in their own words what they already know about a topic, in writing or verbally to the entire group or to a smaller group of learners in a think-pair-share approach, can help to develop better insight (for both the learner and the instructor) into their deeply held knowledge and attitudes. As the instructor and the learner become more aware of this knowledge, they can better analyze existing mental models and, when necessary, adjust or modify them.

6. Self-efficacy and individual control foster motivation to learn.
Humans have a basic tendency to seek to control their environment. If learners perceive themselves as doing something because they want to do it, they are more likely to feel in control of their learning. At the same time, instructors seek to impose structure and organization on the academic environment to facilitate learning. Yet, structure alone will not create an effective learning experience. When learners feel their instructors are using controlling techniques (rather than those that promote autonomous choice), they are likely to show reduced intrinsic motivation, which has been shown to result in lower academic performance as well as substantial deterioration in other important characteristics (Amabile & Hennessey, 1992; Boggiano, & Pittman, 1992; Brophy, 2004; Vockell, n.d.). In fact, the feeling of loss of control is one of the most powerful anti-motivating factors in education (Glasser, 1998, 2001). Creating an appropriate balance between instructor-imposed conditions and student choice of learning activities, on the other hand, encourages self-efficacy, responsibility, and motivation.

In order to maximize motivation to accomplish meaningful learning tasks, and simultaneously prevent learners from being overwhelmed by them, the nature and sequence of learning tasks need to be personalized for each individual learner (Corbalan, Kester, & Van Merrienboer, 2006). Personalization of materials to individual learners' needs facilitates learning by adjusting the level of difficulty and available support for each task, preventing cognitive overload. The task features can also be varied in such a way that learning is promoted.

7. Learning is influenced by expectations.
In many cases, people develop internalized perceptions of their chance of succeeding at a particular task by the information communicated by others. The messages that others send us about our abilities and chances for success or failure help determine external behaviors and have powerful impact on feelings, attitudes, and motivations. From an educational perspective, people tend to perform to the level expected of them, but they may not advance their learning beyond those expectations.

Therefore, trainers must communicate clear and specific expectations of learner behavior. This can be done with the aid of brief agenda at the very least, or a more detailed syllabus or workshop outline containing (as appropriate) clear learning objectives; detailed descriptions of activities, assignments, and due dates; descriptions of accepted social, communication, civility, and academic honesty behaviors; and unambiguous grading and assessment criteria.

Providing a preview of what will be covered in the workshop at the beginning of the experience is another good way to provide guidance on what participants are supposed to learn.

It is also helpful to learning if the trainer communicates his/her confidence in participants' ability to succeed in the workshop and in teaching the seminar. The trainer should communicate these expectations early and often so that participants know what is expected of them (e.g., fairness, enthusiasm, knowledge of the subject matter, timeliness, respect). Successful learning experiences early in the training build confidence, engagement, and motivation for future learning. Once learners develop a success orientation, the difficulty and challenge of learning experiences can be increased.

8. Feedback influences learning.

Feedback is a self-regulating device that allows the learner to correct, modify, and redirect his/her learning strategies and attitudes and enables the instructor to correct, modify, and redirect his/her teaching strategies and attitudes. For both learner and instructor, knowing what is understood and what is not focuses learning. Hattie and Timperley's (2007) study of 12 meta-analyses (which included 197 studies and almost 7,000 effect sizes) assessing influences on learner achievement indicated an effect size for feedback that fell in the top 5 to 10 highest of those studied. For example, they found that feedback offered throughout the learning process enhances motivation. Frequent feedback guides learners better than infrequent feedback because it reduces uncertainty, thereby increasing coping ability while lowering stress responses. But, the timing of feedback is also important. Immediate feedback to correct errors during learning (task acquisition) can increase the rate of acquisition (Hattie & Timperley).

In applying this concept, facilitators must not assume participants understand; instead, they must inquire directly, indirectly, and often. Using classroom assessment techniques — low-stakes methods for gathering information about how students are learning through questions, discussion, and paper-and-pencil activities — provides feedback to instructors about their teaching and, most importantly, to participants about the quality of their learning. Angelo and Cross (1993) provide examples of 50 easy to use classroom assessment techniques that can be applied in first-year seminars and instructor training programs. Individual remote response systems (clickers) use technology to provide real-time assessment of comprehension of teaching and provide direct feedback to learners using graphs and frequency data that can be integrated into PowerPoint presentations. An added feature of using clickers is that learner response data can be stored in computer memory and used to chart both individual and whole-group response patterns, thereby providing evidence of learning progress over time.

Instructors can assist learners in developing personal assessments of their learning progress and strategies through the use of reflective discussion and writing techniques (i.e., learning journals, self-assessment inventories, parallel evaluation forms, and critical incident reports (see Brookfield, 1995). In this way, learners provide their own feedback about what has and has not worked in terms of study behaviors and also monitor their level of learning progress.

Conclusion

The preparation of first-year seminar instructors is critical to their success. Over the past 30 years, the evolving discipline of faculty development has provided valuable information and insight on how to develop such training programs. While there is no universally accepted way to design and deliver training for seminar instructors, this chapter has focused on understanding how people, particularly adults, learn and applying this knowledge to instructor training and seminar instruction. Drawing on this knowledge, faculty developers (instructors of learning experiences) need to design their training programs, in four general ways (Bransford et al., 2000):

» *As learner-centered.* Pay close attention to what learners bring to the classroom, seminar, or workshop—their prior knowledge, skills, and attitudes; views of learning; and cultural backgrounds—when designing teaching and learning activities. They must also focus on the progress of individual learners, providing appropriate feedback and "just manageable difficulties" (Bransford et al., p. 24) to maintain individual engagement and avoid discouragement.

» *As knowledge-centered.* Attend to what is taught (content) and why it is taught (understanding) so that learning can be facilitated and transferred to different situations. Understanding is key to moving beyond memorization and surface learning to deeper level knowledge. Learners need to be engaged in hands-on experiences that incorporate metacognitive strategies that facilitate future learning.

» *As assessment-centered.* Develop and use formative assessment techniques that provide regular, ongoing feedback to both instructors and learners about what and how well they are learning. These progress checks should provide opportunities for learners to revise and improve their learning and provide the same opportunities for instructors to improve their teaching.

» *As community-centered.* Understand that learning is influenced by the context in which it takes place. A learning environment that communicates intellectual cooperation and collaboration versus individual competition will encourage risk-taking and social acceptance of learning. Learning within a community of learners couples the social needs of learners to fit in with intellectual curiosity inherent in human beings.

Chapter 4
The Content of First-Year Seminar Training

Organizing and delivering training programs can be a challenge considering the range of backgrounds, disciplines, and instructional experience of seminar instructors. Further complicating the challenge is the fact that the skills a group of new instructors already possess are varied, so an audit or assessment of the participants' level of skill development can be instructive to planners. For instructors with prior college teaching experience, first-year seminars may differ significantly from other courses taught in a number of ways: learner academic preparation and personal characteristics; breadth and depth of the material covered; grading and assessment approaches; and most importantly, the seminar's desired pedagogy and learning outcomes. Often the seminar represents an instructional venture outside one's traditional discipline, covering information to which the instructor may not have previous in-depth exposure. Moving outside one's intellectual comfort zone may make it difficult to design and choose teaching approaches appropriate to the task at hand. For the novice instructor, first-year seminars can be even more threatening, as often the only experience the seminar instructor has had is from the other side of the desk, as a learner rather than a teacher. The entire teaching enterprise may be journey into the unknown.

The fact that several types of first-year seminars exist complicates the treatment of content and goals of training. While individual instructors are frequently allowed to tailor their seminar courses to capitalize on their expertise, experience, and interests, course administrators may also determine course content. Cuseo (1999) provides an excellent discussion of the seminar's ability, with its emphasis on the learning process and personal development, to provide a counter-point to the breadth and scope of typical first-year survey courses, where lecturing and a focus on covering large amounts of material are the norm. Seminars are usually smaller in size and less content-driven, thereby providing space for instructors to make what is covered relevant to general learning goals and geared toward success of the learner's entire academic experience. As such, content for the seminar frequently focuses on both the academic and nonacademic facets of the college experience (Upcraft & Gardner, 1989). To that end, this chapter addresses several general topics that can be included in most training programs to help instructors design and deliver effective first-year seminars. The authors begin by describing a model for selecting content for instructor training

A Model for Developing Seminar Instructor Training

Having a comprehensive model from which to view teaching and learning can guide in the content selection for instructor training. Groccia (1997) initially described such a model in a newsletter published at the University of Missouri as a way to organize and describe the activities of the campus teaching and learning center. The model also appeared in the *POD Network News* (Groccia, 2007) and in a book chapter on facilitating social justice education (St. Clair & Groccia, 2009) to provide a framework for faculty developers to conceptualize their activities. Additionally, the model provides the organizational structure for a forthcoming book entitled *The Handbook of College and University Teaching: Global Perspectives* (Groccia, Alsudairy & Buskist, 2012). This model consists of seven interrelated variables that influence teaching and learning (Figure 4.1). Groccia's framework extended and built upon Dunkin and Biddle's (1974) model for studying classroom teaching and Shulman's (1986) synoptic map of research on teaching.

The seven interrelated variables are not new to faculty in higher education. But, for many reasons, faculty members tend to focus on one or two of them and overlook the others. The base of the model suggests that the foundation of the teaching enterprise rests upon the intended learning outcomes, while the lines signify the interconnectedness of the variables and underscore the influence each has on the others. In a way, this is related to the concept of backward course design that proposes that the first step in course design is to begin with the outcome in mind, determining what students are supposed to learn comes before the design of instructional or assessment methods. The five variables at the top of the model can be considered indicator or preliminary variables, those conditions or realities that instructors should know before choosing teaching techniques, the middle oval in the model.

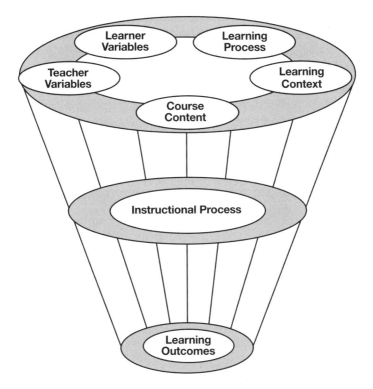

Figure 4.1. A model for understanding teaching and learning. Reprinted from "Planning Faculty Development Activities: Using a Holistic and Learning Model" by J. E. Groccia, 2007, *POD Network News,* Winter, pp. 2-3. Copyright 2007 by Professional and Organizational Development Network in Higher Education. Reprinted with permission.

The first variable for faculty developers or instructors to consider in this teaching and learning model is *learning outcomes.* These are the short- and long-term goals of the training program or first-year education. What do we want instructors in the training program, or learners in the seminars to know, and how will we know that they know? Assessment is a key function to determine whether identified learning outcomes have been met through the instructional processes that reflect the instructor, learner, learning process, learning context, and content variables of the model. Systematic and systemic assessments for each variable of the model, however, are necessary to sustain the curriculum.

Moving to the top ring of ovals in this model, the next set of variables to consider, *instructor* or *teacher variables,* emphasize that instructors need to understand who they are and what they bring to the learning situation. Socio-economic, race, gender, age, and cultural background; academic preparation; and personal characteristics, such as thinking and learning styles, attitudes, and values, all affect teaching, curricular development, and relationships with learners. The more instructors understand themselves, the better able they will be to capitalize on their strengths, minimize weaknesses, and ultimately improve their teaching and students' learning. Training programs should incorporate activities that provide opportunities for instructor self-assessment and reflection to consider these.

The third set of variables relates to the *learner*. Like their instructors, learners' backgrounds, academic preparation, and individual characteristics influence learning. Armed with an understanding of the learners, through frequent and regular assessments, faculty members are better able to develop learning activities that are accessible to students in ways that are appropriate to their skills, interests, and needs. Understanding first-year learners, as previously indicated should be a central part of instructor training and should be revisited over time as additional learner data becomes available from local and national surveys.

The *learning process* must also be understood. The process of human learning has been thoroughly researched over the past 100 years and has been summarized in chapter 3 of this volume. The wealth of information about human learning, and how that knowledge can be applied to enhance teaching can provide topics for multiple training programs over an extended period of time.

Understanding the impact of the situation in which learning takes place, labeled *learning context* in this model, can provide valuable knowledge to instructors. Learning does not occur in a vacuum, physical surroundings influence instructor as well as learner behaviors. Besides the obvious classroom variables such as seating plan, room size and design, and access to instructional technologies, the learning context can include general elements of the educational institution that can impact seminar administration, instructor selection processes, values and goals of the first-year program, course evaluation methods, and learner selection policies.

A critical element in the design and delivery of effective instruction in first-year seminar is the selection or creation of appropriate *course content*. The accuracy, difficulty level, organization, and meaning of course content, what is taught and learned, must be appropriate to the desired learning outcomes, the learners being taught, and the expertise of instructors. Selecting the right content of instructor training programs will go a long way in determining if the training will be successful. The same is true in designing first-year seminars.

The variable that draws instructor, learner, learning process, learning context, and content together is *instructional processes*, or pedagogy. How the training and seminars are taught, the choice of one teaching method over another, should be made after consideration of desired learning outcomes, a careful review of the evidence on the effectiveness of different teaching approaches, the prior knowledge and present needs of learners, the expertise of instructors, and the limits or advantages presented by the classroom context.

Drawing on Groccia's (2007) model, a range of topics for a comprehensive first-year seminar training program can be identified. The remainder of the chapter will address some of these topics in greater depth (e.g., student development theory, academic skills for first-year students, effective teaching), while other topics (e.g., understanding learning theories, classroom assessment techniques) are addressed elsewhere in this volume. Possible topics for the first-year seminar training include:

Learning Outcomes
» Developing learning objectives
» Assessing student learning
» Developing rubrics and evaluating student work
» Using classroom assessment techniques
» Understanding first-year seminar goals and objectives

Learner Variables
» Characteristics of millennial learners
» Learning styles
» Impact of diversity on student learning and behavior
» The first-year learner
» Student development theory

Faculty Variables
» Balancing work and personal issues
» Identifying teaching styles
» Mentoring the new seminar instructor
» Understanding the millennial instructor
» Developing a rapport with first-year students

Learning Process
» Learning theories
» Evidenced-based instruction
» Scholarship of teaching and learning

>> Scholarship and research on first-year seminars
>> The testing effect on learning and motivation

Learning Context

>> Engaging learning environments
>> Influence of institutional type
>> The impact of culture on learning and learner behavior
>> Impact of institutional mission on teaching and learning
>> Principles of classroom design

Learning Content

>> Backward course design
>> Spiral curriculum (the process in teaching or course design where a topic is presented numerous times, each time at a higher level of difficulty and in greater depth)
>> Information literacy (i.e., learning how to access and use information effectively)
>> Academic skills for first-year learners
>> Seminar syllabus design

Instructional Processes

>> Characteristics of effective teaching
>> Enhanced and scientific lecturing
>> Instructional technology
>> Active-learning techniques (e.g., cooperative learning, problem-based learning, case study methodology)
>> Principles of universal design

Developmental Changes in the First College Year

Instructors need to know about the learners they will teach, and the training for instructors of first-year seminars will be enhanced by a general understanding of student development theory. Departure to college can, for many first-year students, represent the most important combination of changes to this point in their lives—changes that occur along four major, interconnected dimensions: (a) physical, (b) cognitive, (c) emotional, and (d) social. Instructors of first-year students should be made aware of these changes and use this knowledge as a foundation for determining instructional strategies and relationships. It is also important for faculty to understand that what happens within a classroom or learning context takes place against the backdrop of other pressures, influences, needs, and motivations. While changes along these four dimensions continue throughout one's lifetime, the concentration of changes within the nexus of the first college year represents a significant challenge to most college students.

Physically, students experience normal maturational changes as their bodies move from adolescence to early adulthood. These changes are further influenced by lifestyle choices involving eating and dieting, exercise and recreation activity, sleep patterns, and participation in sexual behaviors. All of these behaviors can impact a learner's self-concept and self-control as well as academic performance (Groccia, 1992).

Cognitive changes revolve around increasing the amount, breadth, and depth of knowledge as first-year students engage in learning activities in and out of class. This dimension is, on the surface, the prime reason for attending college, and cognitive growth is influenced by many external (e.g., courses taken, quality of teaching) as well as internal (e.g., motivation, self-efficacy and responsibility, study habits) factors.

The transition from high school senior to first-year college student can trigger a wide range of emotional changes, including loneliness, anxiety, depression, confusion, and feelings of inadequacy. The degree of autonomy students experience in managing their own time and making choices about when and how much to study, sleep, and socialize with friends can be very stressful.

Social changes often result from separation from hearth and home, family and friends, familiar places and routines. These changes may also be precipitated by new relationships and expectations. Some will make the adjustment well; others will struggle. Living in a residence hall with strangers can trigger conflict and the need to accommodate to different styles of living, social behavior, sleeping patterns. Forming attachments to others, while retaining those already formed with family and friends at home can take effort and energy. Dealing with interpersonal value conflicts, which often result when people from different upbringings get together, can be difficult.

It is important for instructors to realize that students in their seminars are enmeshed within this world of change. Knowledge of general student development needs to be complemented with knowledge about institution specific learner information. In addition to the question of what first-year learners are like in a general sense, answers to questions such as What are our students like? What skills, abilities, interests, and attributes do they bring to the seminar? and What do they need to succeed? should be provided during seminar instructor training. Training programs need to expose instructors to these learner realities in ways that provide a level of understanding and empathy that can be communicated to students. Appendix B provides a list of online resources that might be used to develop content for or to supplement faculty training programs.

Learning Goals for First-Year Students

Because many seminars include the development of academic skills as among their important course objectives (Padgett & Keup, 2011), a discussion of institutional expectations for first-year student learning outcomes may be an important topic for seminar training. For example, Erickson, Peters, and Strommer (2006) suggest that learning goals for first-year students fall into the following categories: (a) knowing/memorizing, (b) understanding, (c) thinking/applying, and (d) learning how to learn.

> » *Knowing/memorizing.* Most first-year students are enrolled in introductory courses that are focused on providing foundational knowledge that will be elaborated and expanded upon in subsequent courses. They will be pressed to know and remember information such as dates, terms, facts, definitions, and concepts. The most basic technique for knowing on this level is memorization. While most faculty developers and educational experts suggest that teaching needs to move beyond this basic level of knowing, the majority of first-year courses emphasize memorization (NSSE, 2004).
>
> Because seminar pedagogy frequently emphasizes discussion-based learning, these courses may offer a respite from large lecture classes where the focus is on content recall. They may also help students gain practice in learning strategies that move beyond memorization. At many institutions, seminar courses include topics such as critical thinking, effective study habits, personal learning styles, and academic self-awareness, in addition to disciplinary content. Training programs should model instructional techniques that maximize participant interaction and engagement— techniques that will help students gain foundational knowledge without emphasizing rote memorization.
>
> » *Understanding.* Moving learners beyond recall, recognition, and memorization to a greater in-depth understanding is another goal for first-year instruction. The use of examples and illustrations, by both teachers and students, is especially helpful for developing understanding. Asking students to explain how the examples relate to the topics and concepts being studied are an effective way to facilitate increased understanding.

Training programs should reflect preferred seminar pedagogy by providing opportunities to share personal experience and reflect on experiences, events, and issues drawn from the first-year seminar at that institution.

» *Thinking/applying.* Teaching first-year students to use what they have memorized and understood in a way that leads to being able to explain cause and effect, draw conclusions, and solve problems is another goal of first-year instruction. Instructors can help students gain proficiency in application by asking them to solve ill-structured problems, analyze or assess an issue through the lens of class content, or to create something different or new. Free association and brainstorming activities, opportunities to argue multiple sides of an issue, or role play activities asking students to imagine how someone else (e.g., another student, theorist, expert) would solve a problem can also foster thinking and application. As noted earlier, training experiences can model how these activities might be used in the seminar class.

» *Learning how to learn.* A basic learning goal for first-year students is to learn how to learn. Many students were successful in high school but do not possess effective strategies for college success because they were not challenged to develop flexible and strategic study behaviors that would translate to the increased demands of higher education. Carey (2010) also notes that the instruction high school students receive on developing effective study habits is often not supported by research. Therefore, training programs should integrate learning-how-to-learn activities and resources directly and indirectly. Specific topics might include reading effectiveness, note taking skills, time management, test taking skills and reducing test anxiety, concentration, increasing motivation, and academic writing skills (Groccia, 1992). The training program can also model three strategies for facilitating learning how to learn:

1. *Preview.* At the beginning of each workshop, or each unit within the workshop, participants are asked to write down two questions they want answered as a way of focusing attention on the material to be presented. This self-inquiry stimulates thinking, engages participants in the material, and serves as an advanced organizer providing cues to focus attention thereby preparing them for learning.

2. *View.* The bulk of the workshop (or seminar) should engage participants in active-learning experiences. Time on task has been noted as a significant element in effective learning (Chickering & Gamson,

1987). Learning how to assess goals can also be facilitated by a content-plus-learning-skills approach. In the first-year seminar, for example, this approach integrates the learning of study skills with academic content rather than keeping them as isolated, stand-alone behaviors. Including the strategies and tactics associated with academic success (e.g., self-regulation, motivation, reading effectiveness, note taking, concentration, time management, feedback) into the process of learning new content can maximize their impact and effectiveness.

3. *Review.* At the end of the training program or seminar, participants are provided with opportunities for review. This can be done in many different ways, such as having the facilitator deliver a brief verbal summary, asking participants to summarize the session out loud to fellow participants or in writing, or asking learners to describe in one or two sentences what was the most important thing learned and what was the topic or issue that remained unclear during the workshop (i.e., a one-minute paper, where students participate in a free writing exercise during the last minute of the class and respond to a prompt related to the content of the class session).

Understanding the Institutional Context

Historically, a desire to increase student use of support services and resources has been a common goal among first-year seminars (e.g., Barefoot & Fidler, 1996). The 2009 National Survey of First-Year Seminars (Padgett & Keup, 2011) found that "providing an orientation to various campus resources and services" was one of the top three most frequently reported course objectives, indicated by 47.6% of reporting institutions. Similarly, 42.4% of the reporting institutions indicated that exploring campus resources was an important seminar topic. It makes sense, then, to include information about institutional resources and support services in faculty development training. New first-year seminars instructors need to have general knowledge of student affairs and academic affairs offices and of the personnel within those divisions. Informational overviews of units such as the office of disability services, the learning center, the writing center, student counseling services, centers for service-learning and community engagement, student advising, health and medical services, and the library should be included in new instructor training. Also, there should be time allocated to training instructors on how to make referrals appropriately and encourage their students to use these services.

Sequencing Seminar Content

Comprehensive training for first-year seminar instructors should include a discussion and overview of what will be taught in the seminars, especially as it relates to student learning and development, as well as its organization and sequencing. While there is little research on the order or sequence of seminar course topics, Cuseo (1999) offers the sound advice to introduce course content when learners are most likely to encounter them during their first semester. For example, if the seminar has academic success strategies as a course goal, test taking strategies might be offered prior to mid-term and final exams, but a lesson on note-taking skills should be offered early in the seminar as students will most likely be engaged in lecture classes right from the start of the first year. Cueso suggests that faculty developers include an activity or opportunity for instructors to identify the "critical periods or teachable moments" (p. 9) during the first year and then sequence content to match them to maximize relevance and impact.

Teaching Strategies

As noted earlier in this chapter and in the previous chapter, decisions about first-year seminar instruction should be grounded in theory and research on learning. Because many first-year seminar instructors will have had little training in learner-centered teaching strategies, they should be a central focus of instructor development initiatives. Yet, simply describing effective teaching to workshop participants is unlikely to result in the adoption of useful pedagogies. Rather, training programs for first-year seminar instructors should be designed in ways that model desired seminar instruction methods. In this way, the delivery of instructor training (i.e., the process) becomes central to content. Several general suggestions for modeling effecting teaching strategies in instructor development workshops are offered in the sections that follow. A more in-depth discussion of instructional techniques for the seminar is the subject of volume 3 in this series.

Creating the Atmosphere

The environment for the training program and the first-year seminar is nearly as important as the content. It must be a place where learners feel welcomed and comfortable. New student learners expect college to be a challenging place but may be intimidated by faculty members whom they perceive to be experts and authority figures. Similarly, new seminar instructors may perceive trainers as experts in seminar instruction, a type of teaching about which they are unfamiliar and possibly even anxious. In both cases, learners may be reticent to participate in ways that showcase their lack of expertise. Making efforts to minimize barriers between instructors or workshop facilitators and learners will facilitate a more inviting and productive learning environment. It may also increase motivation to learn. Specific strategies for creating a welcoming environment include making an effort to learn participant names prior to the first training or seminar session, greeting and welcoming them at the door, playing music as participants make their way to their seats, and asking for and sharing personal information.

Contacting Participants Prior to the Training Session

Providing training participants details about what they will experience can help set expectations prior to the event. Most U.S. universities now use electronic registration processes and course management systems that make it possible to know who is registered for the training session or seminar prior to the first meeting. Sending an e-mail to learners before the first session meets, welcoming them, reminding them when and where the training/class meets, and reviewing session goals can help to minimize pre-meeting anxiety and create a sense of positive anticipation. If available on course management or departmental sites, trainers or instructors may want to view participant pictures to facilitate recognizing and identifying training or seminar participants upon arrival.

It might also be helpful if the faculty developer were to schedule an individual meeting with the training session participants prior to the event, and many programs, including the University of South Carolina, do this. This meeting can be very helpful in ensuring that future instructors understand program policies and that expectations are clearly communicated.

Capitalizing on the First Contact Session

The beginning of training for participants is perceived as an important marker of things to come. It is critical for trainers to plan carefully for this first session. Just as the first class for first-year students sets the tone for the semester, the first training session or, if not a multi-day event, the first few minutes of the workshop creates an impression that will influence participant engagement and interaction. For first-year students the first class can be "a signal event, something they have been anticipating for weeks. At last, they will find out how college differs from high school" (Erickson et al., 2006, p. 67). Students (and instructor training participants) want to know what they have to do, the explicit demands and requirements of the learning activity (e.g., for students, what they need to do to get an A grade, or to just pass; for instructors, what they need to know to teach well, receive positive student evaluations, and be asked to teach again). They want to know informal things such as what the training or seminar facilitator and other learners are like and what the instructional climate will be like (e.g., Will the instructor be hard? Will other learners be cutthroat or cooperative? Will the trainer be open for feedback and participant input?).

A 2010 article by Meyers and Smith confirms that what instructors do on the first day of instruction is related to both students' and instructors' satisfaction with the learning experience as a whole. They argued that focusing on content and spending time doing introductions were associated with greater learner and instructor satisfaction with the first day of seminar. Meyers and Smith recommended that students get to know the instructor and each other, that instructors focus on course requirements and policies, and that they teach course content as opposed to simply reviewing the syllabus and dismissing students early (an altogether too common practice). Students and instructors both want the first meeting to mean something, to begin to build relationships and to provide direction for the rest of the seminar. Likewise in a training setting, initial learning experiences should allow participants the time and space to network and bond with their fellow trainees, offer content that relates directly to the topic at hand, and provide an overview of upcoming training sessions.

Getting Learners to Talk as Soon as Possible

One way to create a welcoming environment is to get all learners conversing from the start. As discussion and learner participation are essential elements in first-year seminars, modeling this behavior early in the training session or seminar and hearing the learner voice by empowering them to speak early on (even before the trainer or instructor discusses the training schedule or seminar syllabus) can create the behavioral standard for the future. Minimizing instructor talk at the beginning of the training or seminar demonstrates the kind of desired learner interaction and emphasizes the learners' role in making the training or seminar an engaging and interactive learning space.

Building in Reflective Opportunities

As many first-year seminars tend to include personal development and learning-how-to-learn topics and goals, opportunities for personal reflection are essential in both the training program and in the seminars. Trainers should build in frequent opportunities for participants to personalize learning by taking the time to think through what it means to them personally, how they can use this information in the future, what they will do differently with this new knowledge, and what additional information they need to proceed. This can be done by reflecting silently on such questions; by posting responses to electronic discussion boards or blogs; or by writing out such responses on in-training or in-seminar papers, reflective journals, or as part of an end-of-training or term-long reflection activity. Some programs, as part of their assessment plan, provide an opportunity for participant reflection through the use of a survey or questionnaire to provide feedback to the instructors and program administrators. It may be helpful to share this feedback with training participants as part of a 360-degree feedback loop that can serve as a final summary of the training.

Sharing Responsibility for Instruction

First-year instructor training and first-year seminars present tremendous opportunities for participants to assume multiple roles of learner and teacher. Training developers and facilitators can share responsibility for instruction by having learners take the lead in managing discussions, choosing topics to be covered, or acting as peer tutors to other seminar training participants. Miller et al. (2001) and Hamid (2001) provide many examples of student-assisted teaching and peer leadership, which can be adapted for the training and seminar environments. Assisting and instructing fellow participants reinforces learning for both parties: the *student* is often able to learn from his or her peer in a way not possible from a professor or workshop facilitator; and the *teacher* learns more about what is being communicated by having to attain the level of understanding necessary to share it with others.

Being Flexible

There is likely no place during a student's first year where coverage of content is less important than in the seminar. This is also true for faculty development initiatives designed to prepare instructors to teach first-year seminars. Being flexible in terms of sticking to the prepared agenda allows learners space and time to explore topics of interest. Each group of novice seminar instructors may differ from preceding groups so it is important to assess the needs, experiences, and interests of each training cohort and use this information to design and deliver the training program.

Establishing Guidelines with Participant Input

Creating a training or seminar environment that is open and nonthreatening often requires clear guidelines for talking and listening. Participants in the training and students in the seminar need to feel comfortable talking about issues that might be personally revealing or taking a position or opinion that might be controversial; therefore, a discussion about rules of engagement, so to speak, or guidelines for productive discussions should occur early in the instruction. Such rules might include:

» Setting time limits for talking during discussions
» Disagreeing in a way that focuses on the statement and not the person who uttered it
» Establishing policies about activities that may distract other learners (e.g., cell phone use, texting, eating and drinking, talking when someone else is talking)
» Creating procedures for recognizing other learners with questions
» Identifying methods for drawing discussions to a close
» Ensuring that all learners have equal opportunities to contribute

Using Technology and Social Networking Tools

Modern technology provides expanded opportunities for access to learners and learning outside the physical limits of the seminar or training room. One does not have to become an expert, but all instructors and trainers should become comfortable in integrating technology inside and outside the meeting space. Course management systems (e.g., Blackboard, WebCT, Moodle) provide avenues for communication and learning beyond traditional place, space, and time restrictions. Social networking sites (e.g., Facebook, Twitter) provide rich opportunities for trainers and seminar instructors to have expanded contact with learners, and it allows learners to be connected to each other in ways that can support the goals for training as well as the first-year seminar.

Using Stories, Examples, and Personal Experiences

Effective workshop leaders integrate, whenever appropriate, stories and examples to illustrate content and to provide a context for learning that might be more accessible to training and seminar participants. The sharing of personal experiences as a first-year learner and/or as seminar facilitator can provide a powerful object lesson. Personal anecdotes can provide a humanizing element to abstract topics and can serve as a model for learners to encourage their own self-disclosure.

Creating Engaging and Active Lectures

There are times, limited as they may be, during the seminar when lecture is an appropriate instructional technique. Seminar instructors, especially those who are full-time faculty members, may lecture as the primary instructional approach in their traditional classes and fall back on this method in the seminar. Research supports the usefulness of the lecture to transmit information, while also recognizing its limited ability to facilitate problem solving, critical thinking, and the type of personal learning that is at the heart of most first-year seminars (Chaudhury, 2011). Where lectures are used, they must be more engaging and active.

Handelsman et al. (2004) have developed an approach to lecture, called scientific teaching, that can provide a useful model for seminar instructors should they feel the need to lecture. In a scientific teaching approach, aspects of active learning and engagement are integrated by dividing the lecture into segments that combine teacher talk, learner talk, and application. Handelsman and colleagues recommend that no more than one third of instructional time be instructor talk. The remaining time should be spent in active-learning activities such as brainstorming, data interpretation, case study analysis and discussion, think-pair-share, and one-minute papers for learner feedback and learning assessment. Because this model integrates active learning, it will be more effective in first-year instructor training and seminars than the type of lecture traditionally delivered.

Conclusion

Organizing and delivering training programs as well as seminars can be challenging considering the range of backgrounds, disciplines, and instructional experience of seminar instructors. Planning and presenting training activities for new seminar instructors may involve program design skills not covered in one's academic preparation or gained though the seminar leaders' professional experience. This chapter provided suggestions on what topics can be included in seminar instructor training programs and described some general and specific learning goals of training and first-year seminars.

Chapter 5
The Role of Evaluation in Instructor Training and Development

The role of evaluation and assessment in higher education is an important aspect of continuous improvement of a wide variety of programs and initiatives. First-year seminar instructor development activities will benefit from intentional evaluation at two levels. First, when program leadership takes instructor evaluation seriously, it can serve as a faculty development tool, providing feedback to individual instructors that can be used for the improvement of teaching at the individual level. Evaluation of training efforts can also help program directors continually enhance their efforts for instructor preparation. An entire volume in this series addresses the topic of assessment of the many aspects of first year seminars.

Almost every college and university in the world includes teaching as a primary purpose and mission. For something so omnipresent, the evaluation of instruction historically has received relatively little attention. However, as early as the 1980s, Darling-Hammond, Wise, and Pease (1983) found that "teacher evaluation [had] assumed increasing importance" as a result of shifting focus in accountability discussions from program management and finance to the quality of instruction (p. 285). In the ensuing decades, attention has become even more intense with accrediting bodies now pushing institutions to measure student learning outcomes. The authors contend that opportunities have often been missed to use the evaluation of teaching as an intentional strategy for faculty development.

When used as a faculty development initiative, evaluating first-year seminar instructors can serve a variety of purposes, benefitting both program directors and individual instructors. Evaluation can assist seminar program directors in assessing the overall program, student satisfaction with the course, and the degree of success in meeting course outcomes. Analysis of evaluation measures can identify weaknesses at the program level and can help determine areas that need attention, and can thus inform planning for future faculty development activities. More acutely, Chism, Lees, and Evenbeck (2002) suggest that faculty development is "a community activity that depends on constant reflection to assess results and re-conceptualize strategies"(p. 36). Evaluation results can also assist individual instructors as they appraise their own classroom performance and success and can assist them in improving their teaching. Evaluation is ubiquitous in the classroom setting, as Frank (1975) suggested in an essay in *Excellence in University Teaching,* "I am evaluated by my students every time they leave my classroom. Armed with this information, I can adjust my procedures, and sell my product more effectively" (pp. 144-145).

Rather that shying away from evaluation as a distasteful but necessary process, this chapter advocates for embracing instructor evaluation as a meaningful tool in continuous improvement. The chapter includes a rationale for evaluating instructors, describes a scheme that can be useful in considering the many options for instructor evaluation, and then outlines a variety of strategies for conducting this work.

Instructor Evaluation

Evaluating instructors is not simply the right thing to do; it is a necessary thing to do. Gone are the days when academic programs existed in accountability-free zones. Encouraged by regional and disciplinary accrediting bodies, institutions now demand rigorous assessment of academic and student affairs programs. First-year seminar programs are not immune from such accountability, and in fact, are frequently under even more scrutiny than other academic programs. As Upcraft, Gardner, Barefoot, and Associates (2005) observe,

> first-year seminars seem to be held to a higher standard of assessment than almost all other academic courses, subjected to questions about learning outcomes, academic respectability, and their possible relationship to academic achievement and retention that are seldom, if ever, asked about other courses. (p. 469)

Unlike the subjects of the traditional liberal arts curriculum that have been taught since the days of the medieval universities, first-year seminars are relatively new and, therefore, must continually prove their worth to maintain a place among academic programs.

When moving beyond program assessment, evaluation of individual instructors comes into focus as a powerful prerequisite for program excellence and sustainability. The quality of first-year seminar programs is, at the most basic level, dependent upon good classroom instruction and student learning. Assessment at the instructor and individual section level is often mandated by institutional policy. These institution-wide measurement instruments may be necessary, but are rarely sufficient to provide specific and meaningful data to instructors and program leadership. Taking the review of individual instructors and class sections seriously and focusing energy and effort on the process can yield extremely useful data for program leadership and instructors alike. Effective evaluation efforts can lead to quality enhancement, professional development, and the overall improvement of teaching.

Planning for Instructor Evaluation

As with any evaluation or assessment undertaking, careful planning is necessary for solid results. Just as creating learning outcomes for a course will provide instructors an organizing framework for determining content and pedagogy, so too effective planning of instructor evaluation helps program leadership create a meaningful and productive process. Considering in advance the purpose of evaluation, the who, what, when, where, and how will assist program leadership in planning for instructor evaluation. Inspired by Centra, Froh, Gray, and Lambert's (1987) Planning for Evaluation flow chart and adapted for use with first-year seminar programs, Figure 5.1 asks a series of questions that can guide evaluation efforts.

Strategies for Instructor Evaluation

Educators would agree that most individuals want to succeed. First-year students arrive on college campuses with a desire to succeed. Similarly, first-year seminar instructors want to be successful teachers. Yet, when learning a new topic, skill, or concept, it takes time and experience to achieve excellence. Seminar leadership can communicate to instructors that only with experience comes improvement and, ultimately, success. Providing structured opportunities for focusing attention on the factors of success, as well as the reasons for lack of success, will help instructors learn from their experience and move toward improvement Through encouraging an ongoing process of reflection, program directors can create a culture among seminar instructors that will promote continued development and improvement.

WHY?	WHO?	WHEN?	WHAT?	HOW?
What is the purpose of the evaluation?	*Who will do the evaluation?*	*When will the evaluation be conducted?*	*What will be evaluated?*	*How will evaluation be done?*
Individual tenure and promotion Individual professional improvement Research or assessment	Self Current students Former students Colleague(s) Dean, department chair, or program director Alumni External consultant Campus teaching and learning center	Before teaching term During teaching term After teaching term	Syllabus Organization of course Subject matter and material Communication skills Knowledge of course subject matter Enthusiasm for subject and for teaching Concern for students Fairness and equity Reliability and validity of tests and grading Use of appropriate teaching methods Achievement of student learning outcomes	Self-assessment Classroom assessment techniques Small group Instructional feedback Focus groups Class observation Videotaping Simulated teaching Peer review Review of graded student work Content analysis of instructional materials Review of class and student records End-of-term student evaluations National assessment instrument results Assessment of student learning outcomes Teaching portfolio review

Figure 5.1. Planning for evaluation. Adapted from *A Guide to Evaluating Teaching for Promotion and Tenure* by J. Centra et al., 1987. Copyright 1987 by Copley Publishing.

Before serious evaluation of instructors can begin, *teaching success* must be defined. Recognition of teaching success as measured by what students learn as opposed to what instructors teach can serve as the basis for evaluating instruction in first-year seminars. Barr and Tagg (1995) first advocated for this fundamental shift in thinking in their landmark *Change* article. Among the many revolutionary ideas they presented is that institutions should be more concerned with how they "produce learning" than with how they "provide/deliver instruction"(p. 16) and that learning should be student-centered and controlled rather than teacher-centered and controlled. They also suggest that instructors are more effective in helping students learn when they design learning methods and environments for students that move beyond lecture and engage students more actively in the class. In other words, successful instructors have two-way communication with students and have mechanisms that enable them to know what students are learning.

Preterm Syllabus Review

Prior to the term beginning, having instructors submit their syllabi in advance of the first class allows seminar leadership to review them and provide feedback to individual instructors. A review of syllabi can help directors gauge instructors' seriousness of purpose in teaching the seminar. It can also provide an opportunity to check for inclusion of the requisite elements of a syllabus (e.g. attendance policy, grading policy, course requirements, and statement of academic integrity) and an appropriate level of rigor. The syllabus review also provides program leadership the opportunity to make concrete suggestions that will enhance and improve the syllabus as related to learning outcomes and methods planned to achieve the outcomes. This window of opportunity for formative feedback to instructors is narrow, but it is a tremendous opportunity to proactively eradicate potential problems that may arise during the term in cases where the syllabus lacks specificity or fails to meet program standards. Preterm reviews of syllabi serve a significant developmental role in improving instructor effectiveness. An added benefit to reviewing syllabi as a method for evaluating instructors and helping them develop as teachers is that engaging in such syllabus review can also serve as a method for program evaluation and improvement.

Classroom-Based Evaluation

The value of feedback has been advocated by Chickering and Gamson (1987) in their *Seven Principles for Good Practice in Undergraduate Education.*

If prompt feedback is helpful for student learning, then so too is it a useful tool for instructor learning and development. Instructors have a number of strategies available to them to assess their abilities to help students learn in the classroom setting at critical points in the term.

Instructors may want to solicit formative feedback at midterm or the end of major units in the course, allowing them to make adjustments in the middle of the term that will improve the student learning experience. Instructors can focus the formative feedback to meet their own needs and desires for validating student learning. As an alternative, instructors may engage in some guided reflection by focusing on what is going well and what aspects of the class are providing challenges and considering how they might adjust things to make improvements.

Classroom assessment techniques (CATs; Angelo & Cross, 1993) can be employed to gauge what students are learning and are useful as formative feedback. For example, instructors who use the one-minute paper technique could ask students to respond to prompts related to the content of the class session. The students would then be able to outline what they learned, provide a reaction to the content, or answer specific questions about the class activity. The muddiest point technique also allots the final few minutes of the class to student writing, but with this prompt, students are asked to write about what they did not understand, what is not clear to them, or what they feel they need to know more about to fully understand the topic.

CATs and other formative feedback exercises can also be used in instructor preparation workshops and then discussed in the training setting as a model for use in the first-year seminar classroom. Those who have never used them before may consider these strategies somewhat risky or intimidating, but the results can provide powerful information that can be used to improve teaching effectiveness. Instilling in instructors the desire to continuously improve their teaching through the use of classroom-based evaluation strategies will serve well them as teachers and the first-year seminar program in general.

Program-Driven Evaluation

Program leadership may encourage the use of individualized classroom-based evaluation methods but will most likely demand the use of program-wide evaluations across all sections of a course each term. Both classroom-based evaluation that is initiated and controlled by individual instructors to assess specific and individual aspects of their sections and program-wide evaluation (e.g., end-of-course evaluation surveys) at the section level will help individual instructors identify areas of strength as well as those ripe for improvement. When aggregated at the section or program level, such data may guide seminar leadership in creating ongoing faculty development activities on topics related to program-wide need.

Program-driven evaluation can occur at many points in the annual academic cycle (e.g., before, during, or after the term). Feedback at the end of the term, as is tradition in the academy, allows improvement in a future term. Such summative evaluation can also be used to improve the overall quality and effectiveness of the program, the institution, and to reward merit. A variety of methods can also be used during the term to help develop instructors and improve their teaching (i.e., formative assessment). For example, midterm course evaluations can provide valuable feedback to instructors that allows them to make adjustments to the current course iteration rather than making changes only to future course offerings. However, analyzing these evaluations during a busy time of the year can also be very laborious for program office staff.

Peer Observation

Another method for evaluating instructor effectiveness is through peer review. Taking a variety of formats, peer review provides a powerful process for improving teaching. Peer review formats can include a one-time observation and evaluation of teaching methods using a scoring rubric, video-taped class sessions for discussion and evaluation, or the creation and implementation of communities of practice or faculty learning communities. In communities of practice or faculty learning communities, small groups of instructors who share a common interest in teaching improvement are formed and interact over time, coming together to discuss teaching, learn from one another, challenge each other to expand their skills, and provide feedback to one other. These self-directed, guided groups can provide a very powerful experience as they focus on mutual challenge and support.

Northern Arizona University uses a comprehensive peer observation process for their EPS 101 graduate and peer instructors that was adapted from materials developed by Mary Ellen Weimer (Weimer, Parret, & Kerns, 1988). The process involves instructor self-evaluation on four scales (i.e., critical thinking, dedication, promotion of student growth, and quality of interaction). This self-evaluation is coupled with a peer observation process involving six categories of observation items (i.e., organization, credibility and control, content, presentation, rapport, and interaction). Appendix C offers an adapted version of the document used in this comprehensive process of self- and peer-evaluation. Involving seasoned instructors in the evaluation of novice or newer instructors enables program directors to accomplish the review process for multiple sections, something that they alone could not accomplish.

End-of-Course Evaluations

The most institutionalized method for evaluating courses is the traditional end-of-course evaluation (EOCE). The results of such EOCEs can be used by both individual instructors and program directors to better understand where to direct efforts toward teaching improvement. Many institutions use a locally developed survey form containing a set of objective questions that measure student satisfaction and other course aspects (e.g., availability of instructors, use of technology) across all courses. By the very fact that these questions are appropriate for all courses across a range of disciplines, they can only be general in tone and focus. They may provide limited insight into whether outcomes related to specific courses have been achieved. Where the option exists, program directors may choose to use a course-specific EOCE instead of or as a supplement to a more general EOCE. For example, at the University of South Carolina, the first-year seminar uses an EOCE designed to capture indirect measures of students' perceptions of their achievement of learning outcomes specific to that course. One learning outcome for the course relates to describing concepts of diversity and recognizing different perspectives, and it is measured by student responses to the following EOCE prompts:

This course helped me

» Describe ways in which people are diverse
» Understand someone else's views by imagining how an issue looks from his or her perspective
» Explain how my values influence how I relate to others

In addition to using Likert-scaled and other closed-ended questions, program directors may also choose to include opened-ended questions to solicit student opinion and feedback on topics of interest and to provide insight into the meaning of responses to other questions on the EOCE.

EOCE results can be analyzed to measure many aspects of the seminar program and can also be used to assess student opinions of individual instructor's teaching effectiveness. Results can be shared with instructors, providing for them their scores as well as the all-section means. In this way, individual instructors can benchmark their effectiveness in many different areas and can identify those areas ripe for improvement. Analyzing EOCE results also allows program directors to identify instructors who are especially effective in different aspects of course delivery. These instructors can be tapped for leading future faculty development efforts to address particular course concerns or topic areas.

Teaching Awards for Seminar Instruction

Teaching awards *within* the first-year seminar program can be used to recognize excellence in seminar teaching and can serve to call attention to benchmarks for evaluating good teaching within the first-year seminar program. The process of initially creating an award and developing the criteria to be used in selecting the award recipients provides an opportunity to focus on the elements of good teaching. Then with an annual nomination and selection process, these criteria are again used and discussed in collaborative decision making. Finally, when the awards are conferred, attention is yet again directed at the desired criteria for excellence in teaching. Instructors can benchmark their own attitudes, beliefs, and behaviors against those of the award recipients. The self-reflection that occurs collectively in individuals can contribute, in a nonthreatening manner, to program-wide instructional development efforts.

Reflective Self-Assessment

Perhaps the most effective evaluation of teaching, in terms of creating change, is reflective self-assessment. Authentic and meaningful self-assessment occurs only when instructors have an internally motivated and constructed desire to improve their own teaching. The focus is centered more on the instructor as a reflective practitioner and less on the seminar students and their learning. The process of reflection and consideration of the teaching practice is as important as the outcome of what is learned through the process. Program directors can encourage instructors to engage in this type of self-assessment as a method of personal, individualized instructor development. Guidance can be provided through suggested reflection questions, such as

» What did I enjoy about my teaching experience?
» What did I find frustrating or challenging?
» What did I learn about myself through this teaching experience?
» How can I use what I learned in my work and in future teaching?

>> What were the strengths of my syllabus? Weaknesses? What would need to change for future classes?

>> What new insights about my teaching did I gain by reading the results of the teaching/EOCE evaluations?

>> What will I commit to do differently next time I teach this, or any other, course?

National Assessment Instruments

Nationally developed and administered surveys can also be used to assess seminar programs and guide faculty development initiatives. Some can be analyzed at the course section level and can thus also be used for evaluation of instructor effectiveness. The first step is to conduct a data audit on campus. The institutional research or enrollment management office on campus can provide program directors with information about which national instruments, if any, are already in use at the institution. If in fact they are, then additional funds may not be necessary to access the data. The plethora of survey instruments available on the national market makes determining which one(s) to use a challenge. The National Survey of Student Engagement suite of surveys and the CIRP Freshman Survey coupled with the Your First College Year survey can provide information regarding large cohorts of students and their experiences at the institution (Appendix B). These can be useful to program leadership in determining content for instructor development initiatives and course outcomes for the program as a whole.

The First-Year Initiative (FYI), a benchmarking survey designed specifically for first-year seminars can provide detailed information to program leadership and instructors alike regarding course outcomes. Fifteen factors are measured including study strategies, academic and cognitive skills, connections with faculty, connections with peers, out-of-class engagement, knowledge of campus policies, knowledge of academic services, managing time and priorities, knowledge of wellness, sense of belonging and acceptance, usefulness of course readings, satisfaction with institution, use of engaging pedagogies, and overall course effectiveness (Appendix B).

The variety of survey and evaluation processes mentioned above can provide program leadership with a wealth of information. It also provides an opportunity to close the evaluation and assessment loop. The most important application of the data on teaching effectiveness can be used only by the individual instructor. It is their teaching improvement that is impacted by closing the feedback loop. For this reason, the timeliness of sharing results with instructors is of critical importance. While the term is still fresh in the minds of instructors, having the data from these measurement instruments will be most powerful.

Conclusion

The process of section-level evaluation as a faculty development tool is not without challenges. Some in the academy will no doubt view such close scrutiny of classroom management and instruction as infringing upon academic freedom. Yet there are few other ways that are as effective as using teaching evaluation as a faculty development strategy. Section-level evaluation will indeed unearth some less than excellent instruction in a program, and this can be challenging for program directors to handle. However, unless the evaluation of teaching can be analyzed at the section level, teaching excellence cannot be identified either. Communicating that faculty development includes both challenge and support is a first step. Developing a program culture that values feedback and continuous improvement through faculty development will strengthen both individual teachers and the program itself. In an environment of accountability and assessment, the risk is often worthwhile.

Chapter 6
Building and Sustaining an Instructor Corps for the Seminar

Staffing a first-year seminar course can be a challenge on campuses of all types and sizes. Rarely do first-year seminars of any type have dedicated faculty whose sole responsibility is to teach in the seminar program. Instead, seminar programs frequently rely on individuals from other academic or administrative units on campus to teach sections of the course. Data from the 2009 National Survey of First-Year Seminars (Padgett & Keup, 2011) found that among all respondents offering the course, 48.2% reported using student affairs professionals, and 29.9% used other campus professionals to teach the seminar. Yet, faculty are the most common instructors, with 54.4% of respondents indicating that full-time, nontenure track faculty teach and 61.4% reporting that tenure-track faculty teach the first-year seminar. Additionally, 46.0% of institutions report using adjunct faculty to teach the course.

Students are much less likely to be involved in instruction with 5.6% of respondents indicating that graduate students teach the course and 5.1% using undergraduate students. When students do teach the course, they may be part of a teaching team. A large number of the respondents (43.6%) reported that at least some of their seminar sections are team-taught, with many permutations of teaching partnerships in existence. Clearly, traditional faculty do not have sole ownership of seminar instruction; rather, campuses commonly engage a variety of employees and students in teaching the course. In fact, Barefoot et al. (2005), reflecting on Lehman College of the City University of New York, argue that "the notion that successful educational innovations can be realized only with a cadre of full-time or tenured faculty is not supported" (p. 229).

While multiple staffing models may be equally effective, first-year seminar leaders are still faced with the challenge of recruiting and retaining high-quality teaching staff. At the outset, they must develop strategies for overcoming challenges to identifying and engaging the individuals on campus with the abilities, personal characteristics, and flexible situation that allow them to teach a seminar section. They must also consider how to reward and recognize the good work of individuals teaching the seminar. Where the earlier chapters in this book addressed preparing instructors with varying levels of experience and from a wide range of institutional roles to teach in the seminar, this chapter examines both initial recruitment efforts of teaching staff and strategies for cultivating ongoing relationships with instructors.

Recruiting and Inviting Potential Instructors
Defining Desired Instructor Characteristics

First-year seminars of all types have two basic commonalities: (a) by their very title they are college courses with limited enrollments taught in a discussion-oriented format (seminar) and (b) their enrollments are restricted to students in their first year on campus. For this reason, in addition to being effective instructors, individuals teaching first-year seminars ideally should have a set of unique characteristics and attitudes, which can be cultivated through faculty development initiatives; be predisposed to creating student-centered learning environments; or have the interest and willingness to learn new approaches to teaching. Several of the more important characteristics of seminar instructors include:

Understanding and appreciating first-year students. Successful seminar instructors will appreciate first-year students and their fresh approach to college. They must have patience with and enjoy helping students learn about their new collegiate environment and the differences between high school and college. They should understand that even academically outstanding first-year students will not become outstanding college learners by simple osmosis and that it takes time for students to understand the new academic culture in which they are now living and learning. Instructors who are successful in teaching first-year seminars are those who enjoy both the content of the seminar and the process of teaching new college students how to learn.

Believing that teaching is empowering learning. The first-year seminar is taught in a small-class environment where students are expected to fully engage in learning and lecture is not the primary method for content delivery. First-year seminar instructors must be comfortable with empowering students to learn and must be willing to share the responsibility of teaching with the students. Barr and Tagg (1995) challenged higher educators to adopt more student-centered approaches to teaching through shifting the educational paradigm from one with a focus on instruction to one with an emphasis on learning. By addressing learning theory, criteria for measuring success, and the roles of faculty, they argued that learning could be enhanced. Weimer (2002) extended some of these concepts at the classroom level by advocating for learner-centered classrooms. She focused on the function of content, the role of the teacher, the responsibility for learning, the purposes and processes of assessment and the balance of power in her model. The active and engaged learning that Weimer and Barr and Tagg advocate are hallmarks of the first-year seminar classroom. Instructors must be comfortable with discussion and interactive methods, and they must be willing to give up some of the power bestowed on the instructors by the traditional classroom environment.

Meeting campus-wide criteria for an instructor position. Each first-year seminar program is a product of its campus culture and environment, and it usually reflects the norms of other academic departments and programs on the campus. Thus, seminar programs should have stated minimal educational and preparation criteria for instructors that are in alignment with larger institutional standards. Depending on the institution's requirements, the regional accrediting body's standards, and the prevailing academic culture, criteria can include, among others (a) minimum level of educational degree attainment, (b) status of employment at the institution, (c) type of appointment, and (d) required faculty development/training participation. Stated minimal criteria can guide program leadership in recruitment and selection processes.

Identifying Potential Instructors

For programs without a dedicated instructor pool, identifying potential teaching staff is an ongoing challenge. Strategies can vary from taking advantage of institutional structures to adopting stealth tactics. Consideration of the typical career stages within academe may also provide opportunities for seminar leadership to cultivate and develop a potential instructor corps.

Campus structures and processes. Many campuses have some form of a teaching excellence center or faculty development program. Individuals who seek out opportunities and workshops sponsored by such programs demonstrate their interest in improving teaching and learning. These very individuals may well be open to teaching something new, beyond, or within their disciplines. Collaborating with the leaders of these centers and programs to introduce participating individuals to the opportunity to teach a first-year seminar may provide a constructive avenue for instructor recruitment.

Another process that exists on most campuses in some form or another is the selection and naming of annual teaching excellence awards. Award recipients and honorees have demonstrated outstanding teaching and are individuals who may well be in a position to teach a first-year seminar. Likewise, most campuses have award processes for outstanding academic advising. Recipients of these awards have demonstrated student-oriented attitudes that would make them outstanding first-year seminar instructors. Even if award winners are unable to teach a seminar section, they may be excellent resources for instructor training initiatives connected to the seminar.

Using social networking and technological tools to identify potential instructors is also a possibility. Websites such as www.RateMyProfessors.com or student-created, campus-specific sites evaluating instructors offer a measure of information that can be used, with caution, in identifying potential instructors.

Career stages and life cycles. Paying attention to the career cycle of academics provides opportunities for instructor recruitment. Most campuses have some institutionalized orientation for new faculty and professional staff. This is an opportune time to introduce new campus employees to the first-year seminar program, its resources, and its goals and outcomes. Realizing that most new employees will be reluctant to take on additional roles, seminar administrators may simply consider approaching these new employees as a public relations opportunity, simply planting seeds for later harvest.

On the other end of the employment spectrum are two groups of individuals who may be predisposed to teach a first-year seminar. Newly tenured professors are in a unique position to ease up on their drive for research and publications and may be looking for new teaching opportunities. Similarly, professors nearing or at retirement may well be open to the new challenges and opportunities presented by teaching first-year students.

Inviting Potential Instructors to Teach

After having considered where potential instructors might be found, the time comes for developing a strategy for inviting individuals to consider teaching the first-year seminar. Relying on a variety of strategies, rather than on a single approach, will yield the best results in most cases.

Individual invitations. The most personalized and focused strategy is to invite individuals one by one. This requires sustained efforts at networking across campus. Engaging in instructor recruitment via a strategy of individual invitation while time-consuming may be extremely effective. By approaching potential instructors individually, the invitation can be personalized and tailored to the individual's strengths, interests, and possible motivations. Meeting with future instructors individually can also ensure that they fully understand program and instructional goals and objectives. Such individual invitations can be done in whatever manner is the norm for such recruitment efforts on a given campus—via e-mail messages, letters, phone calls, or face-to-face meetings.

Soliciting nominations or recommendations. Another sensible strategy is to solicit nominations and recommendations from individuals who already understand, and perhaps have experience with, the first-year seminar on campus. If the first-year seminar is already in existence on campus, then the current instructors for the course have the most current understanding of the course, the instructional demands, and the characteristics necessary for successful instructors. The instructional cohort is an outstanding source for nominating other potential instructors. Similarly, there are likely a number of excellent former instructors who, for various reasons, are no longer able to teach but have first-hand knowledge about the program. These people often can make excellent nominations. There is also the possibility that inviting them to suggest potential instructors may motivate some of them to reconsider teaching again.

Campus deans and department chairs are also a good source of recommendations and nominations. The very process of inviting them to suggest faculty and staff in their departments will provide an opportunity to engage in good public relations efforts on behalf of the program. A letter inviting nominations allows program leadership to communicate the goals and outcomes of the program. Strong positive assessment data can be used in this process to help inform campus leadership about the seminar's benefits to student success and to the institution.

Academic advisors are also outstanding sources of information about potential student-centered instructors on campus. These professionals hear students' opinions of faculty throughout the year and are aware of faculty whose classes student seek out and those whose classes students avoid. Communicating one on one with academic advisors can yield a list of potential instructors for the seminar program.

A final rich source of recommendations and nominations are the students who have completed the course, those who are currently enrolled, and student leaders on campus. These students will be easily able to identify faculty who have strong teaching skills, are student oriented, and would make excellent seminar instructors. Their nominations allow program leadership to send a letter of invitation to faculty, indicating that current or former students nominated them. This alone, will get the attention of the faculty and may well yield new instructors.

Campus advertising and public relations. Every campus has mechanisms for internal news and public relations. These mechanisms vary tremendously from campus to campus, but include print newsletters or newspapers, e-mail and website announcements, and other formats. Where appropriate, program leadership seeking to enlist new instructors can announce recruitment efforts and feature articles on the program and faculty development activities in campus-wide publications. Likewise, individual departments usually have mechanisms for communicating information to their faculty and staff. With a little bit of investigating, this sort of communication can easily be arranged to reach a large percentage of potential instructors on campus.

A year-round effort to communicate about the program will make instructor recruitment easier. When program leadership make themselves available for presentations at committee, taskforce, and departmental meetings, then recruitment becomes a year-round activity. As mentioned earlier, new faculty and staff orientation programs present opportunities to inform those new to the campus community about the program.

Cultivating Ongoing Relationships With Instructors

For first-year seminar program leadership, recruiting instructors and designing faculty development experiences to prepare them for their initial teaching experience requires significant effort and attention. These efforts are certainly important, but first-year seminar program directors understand that these ventures alone are not sufficient to sustain a quality course. As noted earlier in this volume, faculty development does not end when the semester begins.

Cultivating ongoing relationships with members of the teaching staff can lead to sustained instructor involvement and contribute to their ongoing personal and professional development. Just as learning is a critical ingredient in first-year student retention, so too is it fundamental to the retention and persistence of first-year seminar instructors. The upper levels of Maslow's (1943) hierarchy of needs—belonging and love, esteem needs, and self-actualization—can help guide seminar leadership as they design and implement elements of a comprehensive faculty development program that will engage instructors and contribute significantly to the most important of human needs. The remainder of this chapter examines strategies for creating a culture where instructors feel that they belong, are learning and developing as individuals, and can contribute to the continuous improvement of the program. The authors examine the factors that motivate initial and ongoing involvement in the first-year seminar.

Potential Factors that Motivate Instructors

Motivating individuals to teach a first-year seminar can be challenging. Padgett and Keup (2011) report that respondents to the 2009 National Survey of First-Year Seminars indicated that for faculty who teach the first-year seminar, half do so as an overload course. For student affairs professionals who teach, nearly three quarters do so as an added responsibility. Given that many first-year seminar programs rely on instructors whose full-time job is in another unit on campus, one of the most difficult aspects of seminar management and leadership can be identifying and attracting qualified instructors and then motivating them to teach the first-year seminar on an ongoing basis. The wide variety of factors that encourage individuals to teach outside their discipline, or to teach something new within their discipline, make this aspect of seminar leadership especially challenging.

Intrinsic motivations. Many individuals are motivated purely by intrinsic factors, which are as diverse as individuals and their personal value systems. Some may be drawn to teach first-year seminars because of their desire to teach beginning students. Still others are motivated to teach because of the mission, goals, or learning outcomes of the program. And in perhaps a most basic intrinsic motivation, instructors may want to teach in the seminar program in order to give back or contribute to the institution and students. The seminar program may appeal to some potential instructors because they are naturally drawn to the small-group, discussion-based instruction inherent in a seminar setting and to the ability to develop close relationships with students made possible by such a setting.

Many first-year seminars also are administratively housed in a unit serving campus-wide constituents as opposed to in a single academic department. More than half of the respondents to the 2006 National Survey of First-Year Seminars (Padgett & Keup, 2011) indicated that the seminar was housed in a unit with campus-wide or broad-based administrative functions (e.g., academic affairs, 37%; student affairs, 13.9%; college or school, 7.9%). A seminar program that serves students from a campus-wide administrative unit may be inherently attractive to instructors, as teaching in the program enables them to associate with faculty and staff outside their home department and to explore topics and teaching strategies outside their primary discipline and work areas.

Finding these individuals who are intrinsically motivated to teach in the seminar can be difficult because such characteristics are usually not noted publicly, nor do they appear on curriculum vitaes or résumés. Intrinsic motivations that would lead individuals to teach a first-year seminar are more likely to become apparent through personal interactions and casual conversations. Seminar leaders must, therefore, continually and strategically seek out opportunities to meet individuals from departments across campus who are qualified to teach the seminar. Conversations must delve deeper than causal surface discussions, as learning about intrinsic motivations takes time. Serving on institutional committees concerned with student and faculty welfare, engaging in the development of new initiatives on campus, and participating in faculty development activities can serve as vehicles for meaningful networking. Through developing an ever-expanding network, seminar leaders are likely to be able to identify individuals who will be predisposed to enjoying teaching this sort of class.

Extrinsic motivations are more likely to be structural and public and include financial compensation, career advancement opportunities, and support from department chairs and supervisors. When a first-year seminar program is fully institutionalized, teaching the seminar may also be recognized in tenure and promotion criteria for faculty and in the annual performance review process for administrative staff. For many program directors, fully institutionalizing the first-year seminar to the point that teaching in the seminar program is included in the formal tenure and promotion process is a long range goal, but worth striving for.

In some cases, individuals are motivated to teach first-year seminars because doing so is part of their position description or is built into their performance review process as a goal for the year. Results from the 2009 National Survey of First-Year Seminars found that of those institutions offering first-year seminars, 67.4% indicated that faculty taught the seminar as part of the regular teaching load, while 29.6% reported that student affairs staff taught as an assigned responsibility.[1] When the seminar is an overload, a

---

[1] Respondents were allowed to provide more than one response to this question, suggesting that teaching is configured in a variety of ways on each campus. In other words, some faculty on the campus may teach the seminar as part of their regular load while others teach it as an overload.

variety of compensation strategies are employed, with stipends being the most common. Respondents reporting the use of a stipend ranged from a high of 54% for graduate students to a low of 37.2% for tenure-track faculty. Other types of compensation included release time, graduate student support, and unrestricted professional development funds, though approximately one third of institutions report offering no additional remuneration depending on the instructor's primary role. The one exception to this was adjunct faculty, where 13.7% of respondents indicated that no compensation was offered for teaching the seminar (Padgett & Keup, 2011).

For many types of educators beyond tenure-track faculty, teaching first-year seminars can provide professional development experiences that will help them in their career advancement. For adjunct faculty, teaching a first-year seminar will add another course to their list of instructional experiences. For student affairs professionals and other campus administrators, classroom teaching can provide an additional area of expertise to their summary of experience. Friedman (2004) also found that teaching serves as a mechanism for professional development for administrators. Participants described teaching as energizing, intellectually stimulating, and rejuvenating. They also reported learning things through teaching the seminar that could widened their perspective of their responsibilities, made them more competent administrators, and kept them more current in their fields.

Faculty can also be motivated when they see the benefits that can be derived from new activities. Fidler, Neururer-Rotholz, and Richardson (1999) found that teaching the first-year seminar improved teaching methods in general, by decreasing reliance on lecture, improving facilitation and listening skills, and encouraging the use of a wider variety of assessment strategies. That is, faculty members used new teaching strategies not only in the seminar but also in their other courses. Faculty became more sensitive to, and understanding of, students' academic and nonacademic needs, which facilitated building relationships with students, and felt more confident and committed to their teaching. Similarly, Wanca-Thibault, Shepherd, and Staley (2002) found that teaching the first-year seminar had positive professional, personal, and political effects for faculty. Faculty expanded their skills in the classroom, including the use of technology, and found an increased ability to relate to students on a professional and personal level as they became more aware of student concerns. Faculty also reported feeling more visible and felt a greater connection with the campus.

Obstacles to motivation. Just as intrinsic and extrinsic motivations to teach the first-year seminar exist, obstacles are often in place that keep faculty and staff from volunteering to teach the seminar. For many in academic departments, dedication to the discipline is of upmost importance. Tenure-track faculty may be discouraged by their department chairs from devoting time to anything external to their departmental activities, personal research agendas, or publishing efforts within the discipline. Erickson and colleagues (2006) suggest that it is perhaps "too much to ask faculty to give up their attachment to majors and graduate students" (p. 257) to teach first-year courses—especially one outside their disciplinary home.

In other situations, an individual's primary job expectations may be so demanding that taking on additional teaching opportunities may be untenable. During times of budget cuts and personnel reductions, individuals may find it especially difficult to take on responsibilities outside their primary positions. In some cases, supervisors or deans may prohibit individuals from teaching the seminar because they do not value the program goals and mission. And for still others, balancing work and personal life may make an additional role impossible.

Recognition and Rewards for Seminar Instructors

It is a characteristic of human nature to desire appreciation. Intrinsic and extrinsic factors that attract individuals to teach first-year seminars (as described above) are also at play when it comes time to recognize and reward instructors. Because instructors are typically drawn from across campus where they are employed in a variety of other roles, providing appropriate recognition and showing appreciation for teaching in a first-year seminar program is essential to instructor retention.

Recognition can take many forms. Perhaps the most prevalent and structural form of reward that institutions provide individuals teaching first-year seminars is financial compensation. Although important to many individuals, compensation is not necessarily a primary motivator for instructors of first-year seminars. Individuals choose to teach for a variety of reasons. Recognizing and affirming teachers must go beyond simple remuneration. Some suggested strategies include:

Simple acknowledgments. Many seemingly small or insignificant acts can be especially effective. Thank you messages to instructors and their supervisors upon commitment to teach can reinforce the importance of the first-year seminar to overall student success and retention. A hand written note can often provide even more positive strokes than a formal form letter of appreciation. Likewise, acknowledgement of good work can be affirmed throughout the term as stories of success reach program leadership. A phone call or jotted note tells the individual that his or her good work was noticed and is appreciated.

Formal expressions. More formal and program-wide acknowledgements at the end of a term can express appreciation to instructors. A letter of appreciation from the campus chief academic officer to those who volunteered to teach a section of the seminar can underscore the importance of seminar instruction to institutional student success goals. Similarly, a certificate suitable-for-framing will frequently find a home on an office wall and from that place will continually remind the recipient and his or her office visitors of the important work done for first-year students through teaching a seminar section.

Awards recognition. Some programs have created awards for outstanding teaching in the first-year seminar program. As noted in chapter 5, these awards can encourage excellence in teaching, provide a mechanism for communicating expectations and good practices, and promote instructor self-evaluation. The simple process of communicating the criteria for a teaching excellence award may encourage all instructors to reflect on their own teaching activities and strategies. The selection process and the identification of award recipients can also provide a setting for meaningful discussion of teaching excellence among those involved in the selection process. As an added benefit, the process of conferring the award can be used to raise awareness of the seminar program across campus. And, of particular interest here, teaching awards can reward and recognize outstanding individuals.

Feedback. Chickering and Gamson (1987) offer seven principles that promote good practice in the college setting. One of the seven principles includes providing prompt feedback. This principle is not only effective in undergraduate education, but can also apply to any learning situation, including faculty development. Providing feedback to instructors can present them with useful data that can help them continually improve their classroom skills and their overall teaching and can serve as a mechanism for ongoing communication between program leadership and instructors. A variety of assessment techniques can be employed including traditional end-of-course evaluations, peer review processes, and results from national benchmarking survey instruments cross-tabbed with seminar sections. Feedback to instructors can be achieved via formative processes (during the course of a term) or by using a summative methodology (at the end of a term).

Instructors can also be encouraged to become reflective practitioners and evaluate their own efforts throughout the semester. This exertion to produce internal feedback can benefit instructors as they seek to improve their teaching. Individual reflection can be augmented with small-group dialogue among interested and committed individuals who share a common interest in learning from their experiences. Regardless of which types and methods of feedback are employed, critically examining the teaching and learning experience is good practice, which benefits both the program and the individual instructor. A more detailed discussion of this concept is the subject of chapter 5.

Strategies for Building and Maintaining a Cadre of Instructors

First-year seminar directors strive to develop effective instructors who teach term after term. With increased experience, effectiveness in the classroom improves, and thus, the program is likely to be strengthened as well. The value of ongoing training has already been introduced. This section provides additional detail, strategies, and rationale for activities that will strengthen a corps of instructors.

Community development. One way to create or enhance a dedicated corps of instructors is to facilitate a strong sense of community among instructors who are often organizationally disbursed across campus. Yet, building such community can be challenging given the demands that individuals have in their work. In an unpublished paper written at Wichita State University, Friesen (1994) outlined principles for developing community, which included a common purpose, the existence of a free flow of communication, and ample time for group formation and maintenance. A variety of strategies can be employed throughout the year to build a community among instructors.

Regular faculty meetings, for example, can strengthen the community among instructors; however, the purpose for the meeting must be authentic and meaningful. Unidirectional sharing of information that could just as easily be sent out in an e-mail blast or newsletter will not sustain attendance at subsequent meetings. Individuals must feel that their attendance is important and that they benefit from being present in order for them to make time in their busy schedules to return to the next meeting. Meetings need to feature relevant content and activities that engage participants. Opportunities to share ideas, teaching strategies, and recommendations for resolving classroom problems can help instructors see the value in coming together for faculty meetings. Setting learning outcomes will help program directors plan, engage, and deliver quality faculty meetings. Seminar directors should assess each meeting to determine whether the learning outcomes were met and consider how subsequent meetings can be planned to be even more successful.

A web-based community designed to share key documents, resources, and information can also facilitate a connection to the seminar and to the other instructors teaching the course. Public web sites may be used to share information that is helpful and appropriate for all audiences, some information may need to be restricted to instructors of record. In those cases, an alternate, password-protected site may be useful as well. Some programs may make use of course management systems (e.g., Blackboard, WebCT) as a way to manage course resources and information and communicate with instructors. An online community can also assist program leadership in the development of additional resources for instructors and may well incubate innovation and a sharing of practical ideas for classroom management and content strategies.

Communication. Where instructors are drawn from across campus departments, communication is a critically important element in program success. Finding the right balance of frequency and mode of communication so that instructors are not overwhelmed by and begin to ignore messages from program leadership can be challenging. One strategy is to create a weekly message compiling all timely and pertinent information that needs to be communicated. As such, instructors will be likely to anticipate its arrival in their e-mail inbox each week and may be more likely to read it. Keeping communication limited to those messages that are important, timely, and applicable to all instructors will assist program directors in communicating effectively with their teaching cadre.

Academic freedom, challenge, and support. The notion of student growth and development as being facilitated by a balance of challenge and support (Dalton & Crosby, 2008; Sanford, 1967) has long guided educational interventions. Like undergraduate students, individuals who choose to teach first-year seminars will also benefit from being challenged and supported in order to grow and develop as instructors. Many well-meaning first-year seminar directors feel that if they provide a structured syllabus and teaching resources, detailed down to the individual lesson plans, then instructors will find teaching a first-year seminar easy, will therefore enjoy it, and will continue to teach year after year. Unfortunately, this is not reality in many cases.

Clearly defined course goals and student learning outcomes serve as a foundation for any academic course. Course goals and learning outcomes benefit not only students, but they benefit instructors as well. Suskie (2004) suggests that learning goals help students understand what they are learning, learn more effectively, and organize their learning. She continues by suggesting that learning goals also help directors design programs, communicate with colleagues, as well as justify and assess their efforts. A program with a primary focus on learning goals and outcomes instead of content and methods allows instructors to use their individual creativity to personalize the course for students and have more autonomy in achieving program outcomes. Making a class one's own requires more energy and effort on behalf of the instructors, but the course is likely to be more effective if instructors have significant personal investment in it and are not simply following a prescribed formula.

Expecting creativity, personalization, and autonomy in achieving program and course goals does in fact place more responsibility on the instructors. It also provides a measure of academic freedom to instructors as they determine how best to achieve course outcomes for their particular section of the class. A challenge of this magnitude needs to be balanced with sufficient support. Program leadership must provide opportunities beyond initial instructor preparation activities to support instructors as they teach and to help them continue to develop their teaching skills.

Ongoing professional development opportunities. Making faculty development a year-round and continuous activity, supported by helpful resources, encourages instructors to continue learning and contributes to their retention and persistence. It also communicates the value placed on instructor development to the teaching staff and to other campus stakeholders. Moreover, as the course evolves and changes and as new campus issues that may impact it arise, instructors may need additional resources and support to adapt to the new seminar context. An ongoing approach to professional development may include the following:

> » *Individual development.* Personal and professional development of instructors as individuals can also be a focus for ongoing professional development. The better instructors understand themselves, the more effective they will be in the classroom. New theories of student and adult development, personality and emotional intelligence models, and personal

skills development are but a few topics that can help individuals improve their teaching craft.

» *Content development.* New tools, programs, and resources available to support student success on campus provide potential topics for ongoing professional development. Partnering with other campus units such as a division of student affairs, a teaching excellence center, or an information technology division can help program directors institute meaningful and helpful ongoing development programs that will support classroom instruction. Showcasing some of the most successful instructors can also be a strategy for program development.

» *A speaker series.* A simple way to provide new learning opportunities for instructors is through a speaker series. Experts on topics related to course goals, learning outcomes, content, and methodologies can be invited to speak at faculty meetings or special events. Regional or national authorities can be employed, but may not be necessary. Campuses of all types have outstanding practitioners and experts within the faculty and staff ranks.

» *An annual conference or event* for all seminar instructors and program stakeholders can create energy and excitement. Faculty development resources can be focused to create a very special event that serves a variety of goals and outcomes. Such an event can also help program directors focus on emerging program needs, campus issues, or new initiatives. A single event, in which all instructors are present, makes comprehensive assessment of faculty development efforts more meaningful.

Engaging instructors in program development and improvement. Current instructors are perhaps the most valuable resource any program has. Active instructors understand the challenges and rewards of teaching first-year seminars. Their investment in the program makes them important resources. Engaging instructors in program improvement through evaluation can also be a faculty development activity. Most first-year seminars with a robust assessment program have myriad opportunities for instructors to become involved in program improvement. Strategies—both formal and informal—include:

» *One-on-one meetings.* Program directors can gain valuable information about program effectiveness, culture, and health by meeting over a cup of coffee or lunch with instructors and stakeholders. These meetings also provide a setting for instructors to learn about and better understand the program goals and outcomes.

» *Focus groups.* Program directors can also seek assistance from small groups of instructors and provide faculty development opportunities for the instructors through the use of focus groups. Centered on a particular topic, issue, or idea, focus groups can encourage sharing of ideas, thoughts, and concepts that benefit not only the program leadership but also the focus group participants. As participants in a focus group discuss the topic (e.g., team teaching with an undergraduate peer leader, infusing information literacy into the curriculum, methods for accomplishing a service-learning pedagogy), they gain a better understanding of the topic and become part of a process to improve program effectiveness.

» *Program decisions.* When decisions are imposed on people, there is often a tendency to resist or comply reluctantly. However, people generally are more willing to follow rules and procedures if they have had some responsibility in their development. When instructors have a hand in developing teaching techniques that they will use in the seminar, instead of having these required or chosen by others, there will be greater commitment to making them work in the seminar. This type of involvement also helps program leadership gain the trust and respect of instructors.

» *Task forces and committees.* Small groups of instructors can be appointed to address particular problems or opportunities. Through focused discussion, research, and sharing of information and ideas, members of a committee can work together to help solve a problem (e.g., academic integrity, substance abuse on campus) or seize an opportunity (e.g., instructor recruitment, content development for emerging campus issues). Through committee work, program directors can gain assistance from others, engage them in program improvement, and provide meaningful opportunities for instructors.

Conclusion

Recruiting new instructors to teach first-year seminars is a vitally important aspect of seminar administration. A continual pipeline of new instructors will keep a program fresh, vibrant, and energized. Instructor recruitment is a year-round process and activity and cannot be separated from activities intended to enhance the reputation, institutionalization, and advancement of the seminar program. Having an intentional and well-developed strategy will strengthen the program and provide the stability that is necessary in academe today.

At the same time, course leadership must continue cultivating a solid corps of instructors to ensure the sustainability of first-year seminars. In times of budget cuts and retrenchment, this becomes even more challenging. Recognizing that faculty and staff who teach the first-year seminar are individuals with unique needs and desires is a foundational assumption that can guide comprehensive and ongoing efforts to create learning opportunities, engage instructors in their own development, achieve continuous program improvement, and ultimately yield student learning and success.

Chapter 7
Recommendations and Concluding Thoughts

Those who work in educational settings believe that individuals are continually learning and developing. Further, the assessment movement in American higher education, and more recently around the world, has encouraged, if not demanded that educators critically evaluate their efforts to continuously improve their work. This volume attempts to pull together past research and scholarship, descriptions of current practice, and new ideas to create a catalyst that encourages and inspires readers. Throughout the book, suggestions have been made to those interested in creating or enhancing their instructor training and development. This final chapter offers a set of recommendations for consideration. They are designed to help the reader distill the volume contents and create a plan to put the content to use.

Engage campus leadership in creating and communicating a culture that values professional development. A culture of professional development needs to be integrated into the roles of all members of the academic community, including first-year programs, which must integrate instructor training as an anticipated and rewarded aspect of their work. Programs need to back up the expectation of participation in pre-seminar training and continuous professional development with the resources (e.g., time, fiscal support) necessary to provide such growth activities. This will also require that facilitators and faculty developers themselves participate in activities that enhance the skill and expertise to design, deliver, and evaluate training programs.

Design and implement instructor development that is ongoing and comprehensive. The faculty development learning cycle as presented in chapter 1 can serve as a template for such professional training. Opportunities for feedback and reflection need to be more fully integrated into first-year programs, and program directors need to learn the consultation skills to provide such feedback to individual instructors. In addition, these administrators need to become cognizant of and proficient with various methods of formative feedback to facilitate the continued learning and development of seminar instructors.

Draw on instructor development facilitators who can set good examples. It is strongly recommended that instructor training and faculty development model the type of instruction suggested for the first-year seminars. Training programs should reflect and integrate engaging learning activities that move learners from passive recipients of knowledge to participants in elaborating, discussing, sharing, questioning, and problem solving.

Develop and implement intentional and deliberate recruitment of new first-year seminar instructors. Recruiting instructors for first-year seminars is not an easy task. Program directors should pay special attention to the characteristics that facilitate student learning and then seek out individuals who already possess these characteristics or who have the capacity to develop the desired skills, behavior, and attitudes. They must recognize that motivations vary in individuals and that both intrinsic and extrinsic factors will lead individuals to engage in first-year seminar instruction.

Employ multi-faceted strategies for seminar instructor recruitment. Program directors will need to investigate potential avenues for recruiting instructors and developing a comprehensive strategy using numerous approaches throughout the academic year. The staffing of potential instructors is a job that is never done. Good campus-wide public relations and collaborations will be necessary to yield a steady stream of new instructors.

Reflect campus culture and institutional context when creating instructor training and development programs. First-year instructor training programs should be consistent with the program and institutional context, goals, and philosophy. Connecting training and development programs to institutional mission is a productive and necessary exercise.

Ground training and development efforts in theory and research. Training efforts should be founded on theory and research findings of adult and human learning. Trainers need to understand how to apply this knowledge to training programs, both to ensure high-quality professional development experiences and to underscore their value in designing learning experiences for first-year students. Trainers need to constantly explore new ways to apply this knowledge, taking into account the diversity of students taught as well as the range of individuals who serve as first-year seminar instructors.

Ensure that training programs provide a focus on the needs and characteristics of first-year students in the context of the comprehensive first-year experience. Training programs for first-year seminar instructors need to reflect a solid understanding of what happens in the typical first-year classroom and assist seminar instructors with understanding how seminars have been designed to complement and compensate for these learning activities and instructional methods. It is recommended that training programs focus on the affective as well as cognitive and psychomotor aspects of learning both in the training program itself and in recommendations for seminar content and instruction. Trainers need to model the kind of instruction they advocate for first-year seminars throughout the faculty development program.

Plan instructor development activities that are strategically designed, delivered, and assessed. The organization and design for first-year faculty development programs need to be strategically developed to maximize their success. Plans for continuous assessment, revision, and improvement of such programs need to be more fully shaped before they are finalized. Formative as well as summative assessment procedures should be based on clearly developed program outcomes, data collected throughout the training process, and these data must be channeled into program improvement. It is also recommended that the outcomes of both first-year instructor training programs and the first-year programs themselves be communicated widely across campus. Building allies for first-year programs, especially during financial hard times, is an essential function. A good program that is not known to others, especially those in leadership positions at the institution, runs the risk of not getting the support it needs to thrive.

Embrace relationship building and maintenance as key functions of program sustainability. Instructor training and development is not a one-shot enterprise. Opportunities for continuous learning and development are important for ongoing program improvement. Communicating with instructors, involving them in program administration, and rewarding and recognizing excellence contribute to both individual instructor development and program sustainability.

Create partnerships and alliances with campus faculty development resources. Many if not most campuses in the United States, and increasingly, worldwide have a center, program, or group of individuals devoted to enhancing the quality of teaching and learning. Such programs or individuals often have extensive experience in instructor training and many of the topics presented in this volume. They can be valuable allies and provide helpful assistance. First-year experience programs should seek out such resources and integrate their expertise and assistance in the design and delivery of first-year seminar instructor training.

Seek out and participate in continuous professional development. Seminar administrators and first-year experience leaders must themselves engage in continuous improvement activities around the issues of training and faculty development. Conferences such as those coordinated by the National Resource Center for The First-Year Experience and Students in Transition, the Professional and Organizational Development Network in Higher Education, and the American Society for Training and Development provide valuable opportunities to gain knowledge and experience that can be directly applicable to the preparation of first-year seminar instructors (Appendix B).

Approach rigorous instructor evaluation as a mechanism to improve teaching and learning. Instructor evaluation should be embraced as a faculty development tool as well as a feedback mechanism. The plethora of possibilities for the evaluation of teaching should be considered carefully and strategies used should reflect program goals. A variety of strategies can be employed over time to provide a wide range of faculty development activities.

Engage in assessment of faculty development initiatives. Take seriously the fact that a multi-faceted evaluation of instructor training and development efforts serves as a continuous improvement strategy. Evaluating training events should move beyond satisfaction measures and should be employed at various points in time. Evaluation results can be used to refine programs as well as for justification of resource allocation.

Conclusion

This volume has attempted to approach first-year seminar instructor training and development from a comprehensive posture. It ends as it began, by emphasizing that a first-year seminar program is only as good as the teaching and learning that occur in its bounds. First-year seminar programs have the potential to significantly and positively impact the learning and success of the students they serve, as well as the instructors who teach in the programs. An intentional, strategic, and comprehensive program with a mission to prepare, to support, and continually develop excellence in teaching and learning serves many constituents well. When good instructor training and development programs exist, students, instructors, the program, and the institution all benefit.

Appendix A
Syllabus:
The Teaching Experience Workshop
University of South Carolina

Goal Statement

The Teaching Experience workshop provides the prospective instructor valuable insights into the development of a University 101 syllabus, the fundamental areas of instruction for the course, strategies for active learning, the various campus resources designed for student success, and the unique opportunity to hear from other University 101 instructors as they share experiences and recommendations for teaching within the program.

Expectations

Expectations of the participants in the workshop are that they will prepare for the workshop experience, attend all sessions, participate fully, contribute to the learning of all participants, and provide meaningful feedback to the workshop facilitators.

Learning Outcomes for Participants

As a result of participating in this workshop, we expect that instructors will:

» Articulate the goals, purpose, and philosophy of UNIV 101
» Describe the needs and attitudes of first-year students
» Experience and learn appropriate pedagogical styles and techniques relevant to a seminar class
» Develop an understanding of and strategies to teach the major components of UNIV 101
» Become acquainted with the course plan and syllabus
» Build community as a cohort of instructors

Tools, Texts, Materials, and Resources Needed

» Materials for facilitators:
  » Detailed agenda
  » List of participants with affiliation and department
» Copies for all participants:
  » Faculty Resource Manual
  » *Transitions* text
  » Evaluation Forms
» Materials for workshop activities:
  » Ball of twine for name chain activity
  » Bottled water
  » Camera
  » Compass
  » Computer and LCD setup
  » Deck of playing cards for group formation
  » Easel paper pads (4 count)
  » Easel stands
  » Evaluations
  » Flag post-its
  » Flash drive with all content sessions and PowerPoint slides
  » Food for snacks and activities
  » Index cards
  » Lunch ordered for days provided
  » Markers
  » Masking tape
  » Name placards to set on tables in front of participants
  » Pens and pencils
  » Pipe cleaners for final activity
  » Syllabi from veteran instructors

Requirements of Participants

Prerequisites

» Online application completed
» Interview with director completed
» Qualification to teach verified (full-time employee, minimum master's degree, permission from supervisor)

Preparation
» Assigned reading material sent to participants in advance

Attendance and Participation
» Participants are required to attend all sessions of the workshop before they are assigned as an instructor.
» Participants will be observed during the workshop to ascertain their suitability to teach a section of the first-year seminar.

Outline/Agenda

Day 1 Agenda

8:30 a.m.	Gathering and refreshments
9:00 a.m.	Welcome, overview, and introductions
10:30 a.m.	History, philosophy, and success of UNIV 101
11: 15 a.m.	Understanding today's students
12:00 noon	Lunch (discussion of today's students)
1:15 p.m.	Principles of effective teaching/fostering student learning
4:15 p.m.	Feedback cards
4:30 p.m.	Dismiss

Day 2 Agenda

8:30 a.m.	Gathering and refreshments
9:00 a.m.	Community building activity
10:00 a.m.	Break
10:15 a.m.	Teaching and learning theory
12:00 noon	Lunch (on own)
1:30 p.m.	Greeting from vice president for student affairs
2:00 p.m.	Assessing student learning (grading assignments)
4:15 p.m.	Group time

Day 3 Agenda

8:30 a.m.	Gathering and refreshments
9:00 a.m.	Community building activity
9:45 a.m.	Presentation group time
10:45 a.m.	Faculty panel (Q & A with veteran instructors)
11:45 a.m.	Discussion groups over lunch (lunch provided)
12:45 p.m.	Final prep for presentations
1:00 p.m.	Group presentations
3:00 p.m.	Evaluation of workshop & closure
4:30 p.m.	Dismiss

Assessment

An anonymous response evaluation questionnaire is administered to all participants on the final day of the workshop. Numerical responses are tabulated and all open-ended questions are transcribed. Results are used to improve future workshops.

Future Development/ Ongoing Needs

- » Request to teach process explained
- » Peer leader matching process explained
- » Syllabus building workshops
- » Building Connections Conference
- » Summer workshop series
- » Syllabus due date
- » Fall faculty meetings

Notes

Appendix B
Online Resources for Instructor Training and Development

American Society for Training and Development
http://www.astd.org

CIRP Freshman Survey
http://www.heri.ucla.edu/herisurveys.php

Higher Education Trends and Related Reports
http://professionals.collegeboard.com/data-reports-research/trends

Institute for Learning Styles Research
http://www.learningstyles.org/

Journal of The First-Year Experience & Students in Transition
http://www.sc.edu/fye/journal/index.html

NACADA Clearinghouse: Resources for Advising First-Year Students
http://www.nacada.ksu.edu/Clearinghouse/links/firstyear.htm

National Resource Center for The First-Year Experience and Students in Transitions
http://www.sc.edu/fye/

National Survey of Student Engagement (NSSE)
http://www.nsse.iub.edu/

Professional and Organizational Development Network in Higher Education (POD Network) http://www.podnetwork.org/

Resources on First-Year Experience
http://www.willamette.edu/cla/dean/dtf/Appendix_v.pdf

The Chronicle of Higher Education (and its annual Almanac of Higher Education) http://chronicle.com/section/Facts-Figures/58/

The Collegiate Learning Assessment (CLA)
http://www.collegiatelearningassessment.org/

The First-Year Initiative
http://www.webebi.com/_AsmtServices/FYI/FYI.aspx

The Higher Education Research Institute Annual Freshman Survey
http://www.heri.ucla.edu/index.php

The International Archive of Educational Data
http://www.icpsr.umich.edu/IAED/

The National Center for Educational Statistics
http://nces.ed.gov/

The University of Kansas Center for Teaching Excellence Link to Other Faculty Development Centers
http://www.cte.ku.edu/resources/websites.shtml

Your First College Year survey
http://gseis.ucla.edu/heri/herisurveys.php

Appendix C

Peer Observation Process for EPS 101 Instructors

Adapted from the Department of Educational Psychology, Northern Arizona University

General Instructions

It is imperative that all participants follow these procedures universally. Uniformity will ensure that our end product will be consistent and manageable. Follow the procedures in the chronology they occur.

Instructor

1. Fill out Instructor Self-Evaluation form.
2. Score and reflect on the Self-Evaluation. E-mail your reflection to the director of Academic Transition Programs.
3. Complete and e-mail Made-To-Order form to your peer observer at least one day before your observation.
4. After your class observation, evaluate yourself using your Made-To-Order form.
5. After your observer has e-mailed their findings to the director, the observer will make an appointment with you to go over their observations.
6. After the meeting, give all your materials to the director for filing.

Observer

1. Sign up to observe/evaluate one of your peers. (This should not be a close friend.)
2. The instructor should e-mail you a Made-To-Order form; bring this with you to the observation.
3. Arrive at the class five minutes early and stay throughout the duration of class. Do not leave early.
4. After your observation, fill out the Made-To-Order form and complete the reflections, e-mail this to the director *prior* to meeting with your peer to discuss your findings.

5. After receiving approval from the director, make an appointment with your partner to go over your observations. Try to accomplish this during your office hours.

6. Once completed, give all your materials to the director for filing.

Observation Timeline

August 30 – September 13	September 13 - 24	Before October 8 During next office hours
• Sign up/schedule observations • Fill out Self-Eval form/e-mail reflection to director • Fill out Made-To-Order form/e-mail to observer	• Perform and complete observations • E-mail findings to director/wait for approval	• Once approved, meet to discuss observations/give observations to director

Instructor Self-Evaluation Form

The following are statements describing aspects of teaching EPS 101. Examine the items in each set and rank them from 1 to 4, where 1 most accurately and 4 least accurately describes you or your course. Some items may be difficult to rank, however, it is important that you rank each item and complete all sets in order to accurately score the instrument.

SET 1

_____ a. I am helping my students become part of the NAU community.

_____ b. I am aware of students' needs and am sympathetic to them.

_____ c. I raise challenging/thought-provoking questions in class.

_____ d. I am interested in and concerned with the quality of my teaching.

SET 2

_____ a. I encourage students to share their knowledge, opinions, and experiences (in class).

_____ b. I help students connect class materials to their lives.

_____ c. I remind students to come to me for help whenever it is needed.

_____ d. I reflect on my experiences to improve my teaching.

SET 3

_____ a. My students gain new viewpoints and appreciations.

_____ b. I have zest and enthusiasm for teaching.

_____ c. I am sensitive to students' feelings.

_____ d. I present clear and relevant examples in class.

SET 4

_____ a. I find teaching enjoyable.

_____ b. I make students feel at ease in conversations with me.

_____ c. I stimulate students' interest in the subject.

_____ d. I answer questions as thoroughly and accurately as possible.

SET 5

_____ a. I can detect personal growth among my students.

_____ b. I look forward to class meetings.

_____ c. I enjoy having students come to me for consultation.

_____ d. My students feel that they can recognize good and poor approaches to managing first-year challenges.

SET 6

_____ a. I try to function creatively in teaching my course.

_____ b. I encourage students to participate in class.

_____ c. I actively help students who are having difficulties.

_____ d. Students enjoy the class and find ways to apply it to their lives.

SET 7

_____ a. I meet with students individually whenever necessary.

_____ b. I make adjustments for different class personalities—I try to do different things for quiet classes than I do for hyper-involved classes.

_____ c. I make it a point to be knowledgeable about areas (e.g., majors, clubs, organizations) aside from my own.

_____ d. My students become motivated to study and learn.

Scoring the Instructor Self-Evaluation Form

Instructions (Part 1): The form has four scales. One statement from each set is associated with each scale. Record the score assigned to each individual item in each of the four areas. Total each scale's scores.

Critical Thinking Scale

1-c _____

2-a _____

3-d _____

4-d _____

5-a _____

6-b _____

7-b _____

Total [   ]

Dedication Scale

1-d _____

2-d _____

3-b _____

4-a _____

5-b _____

6-a _____

7-c _____

Total [   ]

Promotion of Student Growth Scale

1-a _____

2-b _____

3-a _____

4-c _____

5-d _____

6-d _____

7-d _____

Total [   ]

Quality of Interaction Scale

1-b _____

2-c _____

3-c _____

4-b _____

5-c _____

6-c _____

7-a _____

Total [   ]

Instructions (Part 2): To interpret the results, look at your highest score(s). These represent an area of strength in relation to the rest of your efforts. Briefly brainstorm four to five strategies to improve your scores in areas that are not as strong as others. E-mail this reflection to the director of Academic Transition Programs. Please refer to the definition of each scale below:

Critical Thinking: This area measures the overall presence of critical thinking in your course. Are you presenting materials that promote critical thinking? Do you ask questions that require critical thought?

Dedication: This area measures your overall dedication to the course and your teaching. Are you an enthusiastic teacher? Do you care about your job?

Promotion of Student Growth: This area measures the length at which you are promoting individual student growth. Are your students becoming a part of the NAU community? Are you providing instruction that helps your student's transition into a successful college career?

Quality of Interaction: This area measures how well you are interacting with your students. Are you creating a positive environment for your students? Do your students feel comfortable with you as a resource?

Made-To-Order Form for Instructional Observation
Overview:

On the Made-To-Order form there are six categories of observation items. The following chart summarizes the categories, noting which ones are *standard* and which are *made-to-order*.

Organization	Standard category: All of these items will be evaluated.
Credibility and Control	Standard category: All of these items will be evaluated.
Content	Standard category: All of these items will be evaluated.
Presentation	Made-to-order category: You will select 3 – 5 items that you would like evaluated.
Rapport	Made-to-order category: You will select 3 – 5 items that you would like evaluated.
Interaction	Made-to-order category: You will select 3 – 5 items that you would like evaluated.

Instructor:

1. Check 3-5 items in the Presentation, Rapport, and Interaction categories, which you want your observer to watch for.
2. E-mail form to your observer.
3. Instructor may ask observer to focus on certain areas of concern.
4. After your class, evaluate yourself with a Made-To-Order form.
5. Schedule an appointment with your observer to go over the observation and compare notes.
6. After your meeting, write up a brief statement on how you intend to improve upon your craft using the observations made by your colleague. Turn this in to the director of Academic Transition Programs.

Observer:

1. Based on the instructor's selections, evaluate your peer using the scales below by clearly indicating your assessment of their teaching. Note: you must assess all items in the first three categories and only items the instructor checked in the Presentation, Rapport, and Interaction categories. Take notes as you observe.
2. After your evaluation, you must write a brief reflection of their performance for each topic that will give insight into your evaluation. Remember, the feedback is designed to help instructors improve. Be polite, but not so polite that your comments become irrelevant. Your written reflection should be two typed pages. Please e-mail this to the director prior to meeting with your colleague.
3. Schedule an appointment with your peer instructor to go over the observation and compare notes. When finished, hand off all your materials to the director for final review and documentation.

Organization *The observer will assess all of these items:*	Needs Improvement			Does Well	
Begins class on time in an orderly, organized fashion	1	2	3	4	5
Clearly states the goal or objective for the period	1	2	3	4	5
Does not digress often from the main topic	1	2	3	4	5
Summarizes and distills main points at the end of class	1	2	3	4	5
Appears well prepared for class	1	2	3	4	5
Appears to thoroughly know content	1	2	3	4	5

Notes:

Credibility and Control *The observer will assess all of these items:*	Needs Improvement			Does Well	
Responds to distractions effectively and constructively	1	2	3	4	5
Demonstrates content-competence	1	2	3	4	5
Responds confidently to student for additional information	1	2	3	4	5
Uses authority in classroom to create an environment conducive to learning	1	2	3	4	5
Is able to admit error and/or sufficient knowledge	1	2	3	4	5
Respects constructive criticism	1	2	3	4	5

Notes:

Content *Your observer will assess all of these items:*	Needs Improvement			Does Well	
Selects examples relevant to student experiences and course content	1	2	3	4	5
Integrates text material into class presentations (uses course pack or Real College)	1	2	3	4	5
Relates current course content to students' general education	1	2	3	4	5
Makes course content relevant with references to "real world" applications	1	2	3	4	5
Presents views other than own when appropriate	1	2	3	4	5
Carefully explains assignments	1	2	3	4	5

Notes:

Presentation *Select 3-5 items you would like to be evaluated on and put a ✓ beside each one you want your observer to assess.*	Needs Improvement			Does Well	
Responds to changes in student attentiveness (e.g., changes teaching strategies, does not let activities lag too long)	1	2	3	4	5
Uses a variety of spaces in the classroom to present material (i.e., does not hide behind the podium)	1	2	3	4	5
Speech fillers, such as "ok, ahm," are not distracting	1	2	3	4	5
Speaks clearly and audibly	1	2	3	4	5
Communicates a sense of enthusiasm and excitement toward the content	1	2	3	4	5
Use of humor is positive and appropriate	1	2	3	4	5
Presentation style is direct, clear, and easy to understand	1	2	3	4	5
Speech is neither too formal nor too casual	1	2	3	4	5
Establishes and maintains eye contact with class	1	2	3	4	5
Talks to the students, not the board or windows	1	2	3	4	5
Selects teaching methods appropriate for the content (activities match well with content)	1	2	3	4	5

Notes:

Rapport *Select 3-5 items you would like to be evaluated on and put a ✓ beside each one you want your observer to assess.*	Needs Improvement			Does Well	
Praises students for contributions that deserve commendation	1	2	3	4	5
Solicits student feedback	1	2	3	4	5
Requires student thought and participation	1	2	3	4	5
Responds constructively to student opinions	1	2	3	4	5
Knows and uses student names	1	2	3	4	5
Does not deprecate student ignorance or misunderstanding	1	2	3	4	5
Responds to students as individuals	1	2	3	4	5
Treats class members equitably	1	2	3	4	5
Listens carefully to student comments and questions	1	2	3	4	5
Tailors the course to help many kinds of students	1	2	3	4	5
Recognizes when students do not understand	1	2	3	4	5
Encourages mutual respect between students	1	2	3	4	5

Notes:

Interaction *Select 3-5 items you would like to be evaluated on and put a ✓ beside each one you want your observer to assess.*	Needs Improvement			Does Well	
Encourages student questions, involvement, and debate	1	2	3	4	5
Answers student questions clearly and directly	1	2	3	4	5
Used rhetorical questions to gain student attention	1	2	3	4	5
Gives students enough time to respond to questions	1	2	3	4	5
Refrains from answering own questions	1	2	3	4	5
Responds to wrong answers constructively	1	2	3	4	5
Encourages students to respond to each other's questions	1	2	3	4	5
Encourages students to answer difficult questions by providing cues and encouragement	1	2	3	4	5
Allows relevant student discussion to proceed uninterrupted	1	2	3	4	5
Presents challenging questions to stimulate discussion	1	2	3	4	5
Respects diverse points of view	1	2	3	4	5

Notes:

References

Amabile, T. M., & Hennessey, B. A. (1992). The motivation for creativity in children. In A. K. Boggiano & T. Pittman (Eds.), *Achievement and motivation: A social-developmental perspective* (pp. 54-74). New York, NY: Cambridge University Press.

Association of American Colleges & Universities (AAC&U). (2007). *College learning for the new global century: A report from the national leadership council for Liberal Education & America's Promise.* Retrieved from the AAC&U website: *www.aacu.org/leap/documents/GlobalCentury_final.pdf*

Angelo, T. A., & Cross, K. P. (1993). *Classroom assessment techniques: A handbook for college teachers* (2nd ed.) San Francisco, CA: Jossey-Bass.

Astin, A. W. (1993). *What matters in college? Four critical years revisited.* San Francisco, CA: Jossey-Bass.

Atkinson, R. C., & Shiffrin, R. M. (1968). Human memory: A proposed system and its control processes. In K. W. Spence & J. T. Spence (Eds.), *The psychology of learning and motivation* (Vol. 2, pp. 89-195). New York, NY: Academic Press.

Avens, C., & Zelley, R. (1992). *QUANTA: An interdisciplinary learning community (four studies).* Daytona Beach, FL: Daytona Beach Community College. (ERIC Document Reproduction Services No. ED 349 073)

Barefoot, B. O., & Fidler, P. P. (1996). *The 1994 survey of freshman seminar programs: Continuing innovations in the collegiate curriculum* (Monograph No. 20). Columbia, SC: University of South Carolina, National Resource Center for The Freshman Year Experience and Students in Transition.

Barefoot, B. O., Gardner, J. N., Cutright, M., Morris, L. V., Schroeder, C. C., Schwartz, S. W., . . . Swing, R. L. (2005) *Achieving and sustaining institutional excellence for the first year of college.* San Francisco, CA: Jossey-Bass.

Barr, R. B., & Tagg, J. (1995, November/December). From teaching to learning: A new paradigm for undergraduate education. *Change,* 12-25.

Berman, P., & McLaughlin, M. W. (1978). *Federal programs supporting educational change (Vol. 8).* R-1589/8-HEW. Santa Monica, CA: Rand. Retrieved January 3, 2011, from http://www.litagion.org/pubs/reports/2006/R1589.8.pdf

Bjork, R. A. (1979). Information processing analysis of college teaching. *Educational Psychologist, 14,* 15-23.

Boggiano, A., & Pittman, T. (Eds.). (1992). *Achievement motivation: A social-developmental perspective.* New York, NY: Cambridge University Press.

Bonwell, C. C., & Eison, J. A. (1991). *Active learning: Creating excitement in the class-room* (ASHE-ERIC Higher Education Report No. 1). Washington, DC: The George Washington University, School of Education and Human Development.

Bonwell, C. C., & Sutherland, T. E. (1996). The active learning continuum: Choosing activities to engage students in the classroom. In T. E. Sutherland, & C. C. Bonwell (Eds.), *Using active learning in college classes: A range of options for faculty* (New Directions for Teaching and Learning, No. 67, pp. 3-16). San Francisco, CA: Jossey-Bass.

Borden, V. M. H., & Rooney, P. M. (1998). Evaluating and assessing learning communities. *Metropolitan Universities, 9*(1), 73-88.

Bransford, J. D., Brown, A. L, & Cocking, R. R. (Eds.). (2000). *How people learn: Brain, mind, experience and school.* Washington, DC: National Academy Press.

Braxton, J. M., Jones, W. A., Hirschy, A. S., & Hartley, H. V. (2008). The role of active learning in college student persistence. In J. M. Braxton, *The role of the classroom in college student persistence* (New Directions for Teaching and Learning, No. 115, pp. 71-83). San Francisco, CA: Jossey-Bass.

Braxton, J. M., Milem, J. F., & Sullivan, A. S. (2000). The influence of active learning on the college student departure process: Toward a revision of Tinto's theory. *Journal of Higher Education, 71*(5), 569-590.

Brookfield, S. D. (1995). *Becoming a critically reflective teacher.* San Francisco, CA: Jossey-Bass.

Brophy, J. (2004). *Motivating students to learn.* Mahwah, NJ: Lawrence Erlbaum Associates.

Buckner, D. R. (1977). Restructuring residence hall programming: Residence hall educators with a curriculum. *Journal of College Student Personnel, 18*(5), 389-392.

Buskist, W., Sikorski, J. Buckley, T., & Saville, B. K. (2002). Elements of master teaching. In S. F. Davis & W. Buskist (Eds.), *The teaching of psychology: Essays in honor of Wilbert J. McKeachie and Charles L. Brewer* (pp. 27-39). Mahwah, NJ: Lawrence Erlbaum Associates.

Carey, B. (2010, September 6). Forget what you know about good study habits. *New York Times.* Retrieved from http://www.nytimes.com/2010/09/07/health/views/07mind.html?pagewanted=print

Centra, J., Froh, R. C., Gray, P. J., & Lambert, L. M. (1987). *A guide to evaluating teaching for promotion and tenure.* Littleton, MA: Copley Publishing.

Chaudhury, S. R. (2011). The lecture. In W. Buskist, & J. E. Groccia (Eds.), *Evidence-based teaching* (New Directions for Teaching and Learning, No. 128, pp. 13-20). San Francisco, CA: Jossey-Bass.

Chickering, A. W., & Gamson, Z. F (1987, March). Seven principles for good practice in undergraduate education. *AAHE Bulletin, 3-7.*

Chism, N. V. N, Lees, N. D., & Evenbeck, S. (2002). Faculty development for teaching innovation. *Liberal Education, 88*(3), 34-41.

Corbalan, G., Kester, L., & Van Merrienboer, J. J. G. (2006). Towards a personalized task selection model with shared instructional control. *Instructional Science, 34,* 399-422.

Cuseo, J. B. (1999). Instructor training: Rationale, results, and content basics. In M. S. Hunter & T. L. Skipper (Eds.), *Solid foundations: Building success for first-year seminars through instructor training and development* (Monograph No. 29, pp. 1-12). Columbia, SC: University of South Carolina, National Resource Center for The First-Year Experience and Students in Transition.

Dalton, J., & Crosby, P. (2008). Challenging college students to learn in campus cultures of comfort, convenience and complacency. *Journal of College and Character, 9*(3), 1-5.

Darling-Hammond, L., Wise, A. E., & Pease, S. R. (1983). Teacher evaluation in the organizational context: A review of the literature. *Review of Educational Research, 53,* 285-328.

DeAngelo, L., Hurtado, S. H., Pryor, J. H., Kelly, K. R., Santos, J. L., & Korn, W. S. (2009). *The American college teacher: National norms for the 2007-2008 HERI faculty survey.* Los Angeles: Higher Education Research Institute, UCLA.

Debard, R., & Sacks, C. (2010). Fraternity/sorority memberships: Good news about first-year impact. *Oracle: The Research Journal of Association of Fraternity/Sorority Advisors, 5*(1), 12-23.

Dunkin, M. J., & Biddle, B. J. (1974). *The study of teaching.* New York, NY: Holt, Rinehart, and Winston.

Erickson, B. L., Peters, C. B., & Strommer, D. W. (2006). *Teaching first-year college students.* San Francisco, CA: Jossey-Bass.

Fidler, P. P., Neururer-Rotholz, J., & Richardson, S. (1999). Teaching the freshman seminar: Its effectiveness in promoting faculty development. *Journal of The First-Year Experience & Students in Transition, 11*(2), 59-74.

Finkelstein, M. J., Seal, R. K., & Schuster, J. H. (1998). *The new academic generation: A profession in transformation.* Baltimore, MD: The Johns Hopkins University Press.

Francis, J. B. (1975). How do we get there from here? Program design for faculty development. *Journal of Higher Education, 46*(6), 719-732.

Frank, G. W. (1975). On my honor I will... In T. H. Buxton & K. S. Prichard (Eds.), *Excellence in university teaching: New essays* (pp. 140-146). Columbia, SC: The University of South Carolina Press.

Friedman, D. B. (2004). University administrators' perceptions of their teaching roles. *Dissertation Abstracts International, 65*(1), 83A. (UMI No. AAI3118410)

Friedman, T. (2007). *The world is flat 3.0: A brief history of the twenty-first century.* New York, NY: Picador.

Friesen, W. S. (1994). *Principles for developing community.* Unpublished paper, Wichita State University.

Gaff, J. G., & Simpson, R. D. (1994). Faculty development in the United States. *Innovative Higher Education, 18*(3), 167-176.

Gardner, J. N. (1981). Developing faculty as facilitators and mentors. In V. A. Harren, M. H. Daniels, & J. N. Buch (Eds.), *Facilitating students career development* (New Directions for Student Services, No. 14, pp. 67-80). San Francisco, CA: Jossey-Bass.

Gardner, J. N. (1992). *Freshman seminar instructor training: Guidelines for design and implementation.* Columbia, SC: University of South Carolina, National Resource Center for The Freshman Year Experience.

Gillespie, K. H., Hilson, L. R., & Wadsworth, E. C. (Eds.). (2002). *A guide to faculty development: Practical advice, examples, and resources.* Bolton, MA: Anker Publishing.

Glasser, W. (1998). *The quality school: Managing students without coercion.* New York, NY: HarperPerennial.

Glasser, W. (2001). *Choice theory in the classroom.* New York, NY: Quill.

Groccia, J. E. (1992). *The college success book: A whole-student approach to academic excellence.* Lakewood, CO: Glenbridge.

Groccia, J. E. (1997). A model for understanding teaching and learning. *Chalkboard, 15,* 2–3. Columbia: Program for Excellence in Teaching, University of Missouri.

Groccia, J. E. (2004). A model of learner engagement. In J. Burns, J. Groccia, S. Hamid, & C. Staley, *Creating engaged learning environments for today's students.* [Teleconference No. 2. Resource Packet] Columbia, SC: University of South Carolina, National Resource Center for The First-Year Experience & Students in Transition.

Groccia, J. E. (2007, Winter). Planning faculty development activities: Using a holistic teaching and learning model. *POD Network News, 1,* 3.

Groccia, J. E. (2010). Why faculty development? Why now? In A. Saroyan & M. Frenay (Eds.), *Building teaching capacities in higher education: A comprehensive international model* (pp. 1-20). Sterling, VA: Stylus.

Groccia, J. E., Alsudairy, M. T., & Buskist, W. (2012). *The handbook of college and university teaching: Global perspectives.* Los Angeles, CA: Sage.

Groccia, J. E., & Fink, L. D. (2008). *Faculty development and institutional quality: Creating the link.* Presentation at the 2008 International Consortium for Educational Development (ICED) Conference. Salt Lake City, UT.

Hake, R. (1998). Interactive-engagement vs. traditional methods: A six-thousand-student survey of mechanics test data for introductory physics courses. *American Journal of Physics, 66,* 64-74.

Hamid, S. L. (Ed.). (2001). *Peer leadership: A primer on program essentials* (Monograph No. 32). Columbia, SC: University of South Carolina, National Resource Center for The First-Year Experience and Students in Transition.

Handelsman, J., Ebert-May, D., Beichner, R., Bruns, P., Chang, A., DeHaan, R., Gentile, J., ... Wood, W. B. (2004). Scientific teaching. *Science, 304,* 521-522.

Hattie, J., & Timperley, H. (2007). The power of feedback. *Review of Educational Research, 77*(1), 81-112.

Hill, P. (1985). *The rationale for learning communities and learning community models* (Report No. JC 890 389). Olympia, WA: Washington Center for Improving the Quality of Undergraduate Education. (ERIC Document Reproduction Services No. ED 309 818)

Hunter, M. S., & Cuseo, J. B. (1999). Ensuring the success of faculty training workshops. In M. S. Hunter, & T. L. Skipper (Eds.), *Solid foundations: Building success for first-year seminars through instructor training and development* (Monograph No. 29, pp. 73-83). Columbia, SC: University of South Carolina, National Resource Center for The First-Year Experience and Students in Transition.

Ingleton, C. (1999). Emotions in learning: a neglected dynamic. *Proceedings of HERDSA Annual International Conference.* Retrieved December 16, 2010, from http://www.greatschools.org/parenting/teaching-values/the-role-of-emotions-in-learning.gs?content=751

Kirkpatrick, D. L., & Kirkpatrick, J. D. (2006). *Evaluating training programs.* San Francisco, CA: Berrett-Kohler Publishers.

Knight, W. E. (n.d.). *Learning communities, first year programs and their effectiveness: The role of the IR Office.* Bowling Green, OH: Bowling Green State University. Retrieved from http://www.bgsu.edu/downloads/finance/file21345.pdf.

Knowles, M. S, Holton, E. F., & Swanson, R. A. (2005). *The adult learner: The definitive classic in adult education and human resource development* (6th ed.). Burlington, MA: Elsevier.

Kolb, D. A. (1981). Learning styles and disciplinary differences. In A. W. Chickering & Associates, *The modern American college: Responding to the new realities of diverse students and a changing society* (pp. 232-255). San Francisco, CA: Jossey-Bass.

Kuh, G. D. (2003). *The National Survey of Student Engagement: Conceptual framework and overview of psychometric properties.* Bloomington, IN: Indiana University Center for Postsecondary Research and Planning. Retrieved March 17, 2010 from http://nsse.iub.edu/pdf/conceptual_framework_2003.pdf.

Lacy, W. B. (1978). Interpersonal relationships as mediators of structural effects: College student socialization in a traditional and an experimental university environment. *Sociology of Education, 51,* 201-211.

Levine, J., & Tompkins, D. (1996). Making learning communities work: Seven lessons from Temple University. *AAHE Bulletin, 39*(7), 3-7.

Lewis, K. G. (1996). Faculty development in the United States: A brief history. *International Journal for Academic Development, 13*(1), 67-77.

Lopatto, D. (2004). Survey of Undergraduate Research Experiences (SURE): First findings. *Cell Biology Education, 3*, 270-277.

Maslow, A. H. (1943). A theory of human motivation. *Psychological Review, 50*, 370-396.

Maslow, A. (1999). *Toward a psychology of being*. (3rd ed.). New York, NY: Wiley.

Mathis, B. C. (1981). [Review of the book *Academic culture and faculty development*, by M. Freedman]. *Journal of Higher Education, 52*(2), 204-206.

Matthews, R., Smith, B. L., MacGregor, J., & Gabelnick. F. (1996). Learning communities: A structure for educational coherence. *Liberal Education, 28*(3), 4-9.

McKeachie, W. J., & Svinicki, M. (2006). *McKeachie's teaching tips: Strategies, research, and theory for college and university teachers* (12th ed.). Boston, MA: Houghton Mifflin.

McNamara, C. (2010). *Evaluating training and results*. Retrieved from http://managementhelp.org/trngdev/evaluate/evaluate.htm

Meyers, S., & Smith, B. C. (2010). First day of class: How should instructors use class time? In J. E. Miller & J. E. Groccia (Eds.), *To improve the academy* (Vol. 29, pp. 147-159). San Francisco, CA: Jossey-Bass.

Miller, J. E., Groccia, J. E., & Miller, M. S. (Eds.). (2001). *Student-assisted teaching: A guide to faculty-student teamwork*. Bolton, MA: Anker.

Miller, J. E., Wilkes, J. M., & Cheetham, R. D. (1993). Tradeoffs in student satisfaction: Is the "perfect" course an illusion? *Journal on Excellence in College Teaching, 4, 27-47.*

National Research Council. (2003). *Improving undergraduate instruction in science, technology, engineering, and mathematics: Report of a workshop*. Washington, DC: The National Academies Press.

National Survey of Student Engagement (NSSE). (2004). *Overview*. Bloomington, IN: Indiana University, Center for Postsecondary Research. Retrieved from http://nsse.iub.edu/pdf/2004_inst_report/overview.pdf

Nickols, F. (2000*). Evaluating training: There is no 'cookbook' approach*. Retrieved from http://www.nickols.us/evaluating_training.htm.

Nilson, L. B. (2010). *Teaching at its best: A research-based resource for college instructors* (3rd ed.). San Francisco, CA: Jossey-Bass.

Nyquist, J. D, & Woodford, B. J. (2000). *Re-envisioning the PhD. What concerns do we have?* Seattle, WA: University of Washington. Retrieved from Center for Instructional Development and Research website: http://www.grad.washington.edu/envision/PDF/ConcernsBrief.pdf

Pace, C. (1980). Measuring the quality of student effort. *Current Issues in Higher Education, 2*, 10-16.

Padgett, R. D., & Keup, J. R (2011). *2009 National Survey of First-Year Seminars: Ongoing efforts to support students in transition* (Research Reports on College Transitions No. 2). Columbia, SC: University of South Carolina, National Resource Center for The First-Year Experience and Students in Transition.

Paivio, A. (1986). *Mental representations: A dual coding approach*. Oxford, England: Oxford University Press.

Pascarella, E. T., & Terenzini, P. T. (1991). *How college affects students: Findings and insights from twenty years of research*. San Francisco, CA: Jossey-Bass.

Pascarella, E. T., Seifert, T. A., & Whitt, E. J. (2008). Effective instruction and college student persistence. In J. M. Braxton (Ed.), *The role of the classroom in college student persistence* (New Directions for Teaching and Learning, No. 115, pp. 55-70). San Francisco, CA: Jossey-Bass.

Professional and Organizational Development Network in Higher Education (POD Network). (2011a). *What is faculty development?* Retrieved February 11, 2011, from http://www.podnetwork.org/development.htm

Professional and Organizational Development Network in Higher Education (POD Network). (2011b). *Faculty development definitions*. Retrieved February 11, 2011, from http://www.podnetwork.org/faculty_development/definitions.htm

Purkey, W. W., & Novak, J. M. (2008). *Fundamentals of invitational education*. Kennesaw, GA: International Alliance for Invitational Education.

Rischard, J. F. (2002). *High noon: Twenty global issues, twenty years to solve them*. New York, NY: Basic Books.

Rogers, C. (1961). *On becoming a person: A therapist's view of psychotherapy*. London: Constable.

Sagendorf, K. S. (2007). *Background experience, time allocation, time on teaching and perceived support of early-career college science faculty*. Unpublished doctoral dissertation, Syracuse University.

Sanford, N. (1967). *Where colleges fail: A study of the student as a person*. San Francisco, CA: Jossey-Bass.

Scannell, E. E., & Newstrom, J. W. (1994). *The complete games trainers play: 287 ready-to-use training games plus the trainer's resource kit*. New York, NY: McGraw-Hill.

Schaeffer, G., Epting, K., Zinn, T., & Buskist, W. (2003). Student and faculty perceptions of effective teaching: A successful replication. *Teaching of Psychology, 30*, 133-136.

Schroeder, C. C., & Hurst, J. C. (1996). Designing learning environments that integrate curricular and cocurricular experiences. *Journal of College Student Development, 37*(2), 174-181.

Searleman, A., & Herrmann, D. (1994). *Memory from a broader perspective*. New York, NY: McGraw-Hill.

Segall, M. H., Dasen, P. R., Berry, J. W., & Poortinga, Y. H. (1990). *Human behavior in global perspective: An introduction to cross-cultural psychology*. New York, NY: Pergamon Press.

Shulman, L. S. (1986). Paradigms and research programs in the study of teaching: A contemporary perspective. In M. C. Wittrock (Ed.), *Handbook of research on teaching* (3rd ed., pp. 6-9). New York, NY: Macmillian.

Silberman, M. (1996) *Active learning: 101 strategies to teach any subject*. Needham Heights, MA: Simon & Schuster.

Skeff, K. M. (n.d.). *Successful models of faculty development: Train the trainer model*. Retrieved from http://www.academicpeds.org/education/nutsandbolts/pdfs/skeff.pdf

Smith, B. L. (1991). Taking structure seriously: The learning community model. *Liberal Education, 77*(2), 42-48.

Smith, B. L. (1993). Creating learning communities. *Liberal Education, 79*(4), 32-39.

Snowman, J., McCown, R., & Biehler, R. (2009). *Psychology applied to teaching* (12th ed.). Boston, MA: Houghton Mifflin.

Sorcinelli, M. D., Austin, A. E., Eddy, P. L., & Beach, A. L. (2006). *Creating the future of faculty development: Learning from the past, understanding the present*. Bolton, MA: Anker.

Sousa, D. A. (1995). *How the brain learns*. Reston, VA: The National Association of Secondary School Principals.

St. Clair, K. L., & Groccia, J. E. (2010). Change to social justice education: A higher education strategy. In K. Skubilowski, C. Wright, & R. Graf (Eds.), *Social justice education: Inviting faculty to transform their institutions* (pp. 70-84). Sterling, VA: Stylus Publishing.

Suskie, L. (2004). *Assessing student learning: A common sense guide*. Boston, MA: Anker Publishing.

Svinicki, M. & McKeachie, W. J. (2010). *McKeachie's teaching tips: Strategies, research, and theory for college and university teachers* (13th ed.). Belmont, CA: Wadsworth.

Tinto, V. (1994). *Learning communities, collaborative learning, and the pedagogy of educational citizenship*. Chicago. IL: National Association of State Universities and Land-Grant Colleges.

Tinto, V., & Love, A. G. (1995). *Longitudinal study of learning communities at La-Guardia Community College* (Report No. JC 950 169). University Park, PA: National Center on Postsecondary Teaching, Learning and Assessment. (ERIC Document Reproduction Services No. ED 309 818)

Tinto, V., Russo, P., & Kadel, S. (1994). Constructing educational communities: Increasing retention in challenging circumstances. *Community College Journal, 64,* 26-30.

Tuckman, B. (1965). Developmental sequence in small groups. *Psychological Bulletin, 63*(6), 384-399.

University 101. (n.d.). *History of the first-year seminar & University 101 program.* Retrieved from the University 101 website: http://www.sc.edu/univ101/aboutus/history.html

Upcraft, M. L., & Gardner, J. N. (1989). A comprehensive approach to enhancing freshman success. In M. L. Upcraft, J. N. Gardner, & Associates, *The freshman year experience* (pp. 1-12). San Francisco, CA: Jossey-Bass.

Upcraft, M. L., Gardner, J. N., Barefoot B. O., & Associates. (2005). *Challenging and supporting the first-year student: A handbook for improving the first year of college.* San Francisco, CA: Jossey-Bass.

Vekiri, I. (2002). What is the value of graphical displays in learning? *Educational Psychology Review, 14*(3), 261-312.

Vockell, E. (n.d.). *Educational psychology: A practical approach.* Retrieved February 16, 2011, from http://education.calumet.purdue.edu/vockell/edPsybook/Edpsy5/Edpsy5_control.htm

Wanca-Thibault, M., Shepherd, M., & Staley, C. (2002). Personal, professional, and political effects of teaching a first-year seminar: A faculty census. *Journal of The First-Year Experience & Students in Transition, 14*(1), 23-40.

Weimer, M. (2002). *Learner-centered teaching: Five key changes to practice.* San Francisco, CA: Jossey-Bass.

Weimer, M. E., Parret, J. L., & Kerns, M. M. (1988). *How am I teaching? Forms and activities for acquiring instructional input.* Madison, WI: Magna Publications.

Wenger, E. (1998). *Communities of practice: Learning, meaning, and identity.* Cambridge, UK: Cambridge University Press.

World Health Organization. (1998). *The 10-step process for developing training courses.* Retrieved from http://whqlibdoc.who.int/hq/2005/WHO_HTM_TB_2005.354_part1_eng.pdf

Index

NOTE: Page numbers with italicized *f* indicate figures.

B

C

D

E

F

J

K

L

M

Made-To Order form, for peer observation, 101, 106–110
Maslow, A., 38–39, 78–79
massed practice, spaced practice vs., 32
materials. See resources and publications
McKeachie, W. J., 5
McNamara, C., 26
meaning, desire for, 40
meetings, regular, for seminar instructors, 18
memorizing vs. knowing, for first-year students, 52
memory, human, 30–31, 31*f*, 33
mentoring programs, establishing, 37
Meyers, S., 57
midterm course evaluations, 67
Miller, J. E., 5, 36, 37, 58
Miller, M. S., 5, 37
mind maps, 33
motivation of instructors, factors in, 79–82
motivation to learn, 29, 41, 42–43
muddiest point technique, 66
mutual adaptation to innovations, 16

N

NACADA Clearinghouse: Resources for Advising First-Year Students, 99
national assessment instruments, 70–71
National Center for Educational Statistics, 100
national or international networks, encouraging participation in, 17–18
National Resource Center for The First-Year Experience and Students in Transition, 94, 99
National Survey of First-Year Seminars
    on extrinsic motivators for instructors, 80–81
    on instructor training programs, 13
    on instructor types, 73
    on intrinsic motivators for instructors, 79–80
    on orientation to campus resources and services, 54
    on overload courses for faculty in, 79
National Survey of Student Engagement (NSSE), 4, 70, 99
need to know, of adult learners, 28
needs, Maslow's hierarchy of, 78–79
Neururer-Rotholz, J., 81
newly-hired faculty and professional staff, as potential instructors, 76

About the Authors

James E. Groccia is the director of the Biggio Center for the Enhancement of Teaching and Learning and associate professor in the Department of Educational Foundations, Leadership and Technology at Auburn University. He is a 2011-2012 Fulbright Scholar at the University of Tartu in Estonia and formerly served as president of the Professional and Organizational Development Network in Higher Education (POD Network), the world's largest faculty and educational development organization. Groccia received his doctorate in educational psychology and guidance from the University of Tennessee.

Over his career, Groccia has directed psychological and career counseling, health, and orientation services and has coordinated faculty and educational development programs at Auburn University, the University of Missouri-Columbia, and Worcester Polytechnic Institute. He served for two years as assistant dean of the Graduate School at Missouri prior to going to Auburn in 2003. Groccia has presented at dozens of national and international conferences, conducted hundreds of workshops worldwide, served as an advisor and consultant to institutions nationally and abroad, and authored numerous articles and book chapters on teaching and learning issues.

Groccia is the author of *The College Success Book: A Whole-Student Approach to Academic Excellence* (1992) and co-editor of *On Becoming a Productive University: Strategies for Reducing Costs and Increasing Quality in Higher Education* (2005); *Student Assisted Teaching: A Guide to Faculty-Student Teamwork* (2001); and *Enhancing Productivity: Administrative, Instructional, and Technological Strategies* (1998). He has recently co-edited *To Improve the Academy,* Volumes 29 and 30 (both 2011), and *Evidence-Based Teaching* (2011). One additional co-edited book, *The Handbook of University Teaching and Learning: Global Perspectives* will be published in the winter of 2012.

Mary Stuart Hunter is the associate vice president and executive director for University 101 Programs and the National Resource Center for The First-Year Experience and Students in Transition at the University of South Carolina, Hunter's work centers on providing educators with resources to develop personal and professional skills while creating and refining innovative programs to increase undergraduate student learning and success. She was honored in May 2010 with an honorary doctor of Humane Letters by her alma mater, Queens University of Charlotte; in April 2010 with the Outstanding Leadership in the Field Award from the Division of Student Affairs and Academic Support at the University of South Carolina; in 2006 as the Outstanding Campus Partner by South Carolina's University Housing division; and in 2001 as the Outstanding Alumnae by South Carolina's Department of Higher Education and Student Affairs. She recently authored the nomination packet that earned the University of South Carolina's University 101 Program Faculty Development Program the 2011 NASPA Excellence Awards Category Gold Award and overall Silver Award.

Her most recent publications include *Helping Sophomores Succeed: Understanding and Improving the Second-Year Experience* (2010), *Academic Advising: New Insights for Teaching and Learning in the First Year* (2007), "The First-Year Experience: An Analysis of Issues and Resources" in AAC& U's *Peer Review* (2006), "Could Fixing Academic Advising Fix Higher Education?" in *About Campus* (2004), and "The Second-Year Experience: Turning Attention to the Academy's Middle Children" in *About Campus* (2006).